THE LITTLE GUIDES

DESSERTS

THE LITTLE GUIDES

DESSERTS

FOG CITY PRESS

Published by Fog City Press
814 Montgomery Street
San Francisco, CA 94133 USA
Reprinted in 2003

Chief Executive Officer: John Owen
President: Terry Newell
Publisher: Lynn Humphries
Managing Editor: Angela Handley
Design Manager: Helen Perks
Editorial Coordinator: Kiren Thandi
Editorial Assistants: Jennifer Losco, Tessy Grabo
Production Manager: Caroline Webber
Production Coordinator: James Blackman
Sales Manager: Emily Jahn
Vice President International Sales: Stuart Laurence

Project Designer: Jacqueline Richards

A catalog record for this book is available from
the Library of Congress, Washington, DC

ISBN 1 877019 64 X

Color reproduction by Colourscan Co Pte Ltd
Printed by SNP LeeFung (China)
Printed in China

A Weldon Owen Production

CONTENTS

PART TWO
DESSERT RECIPES

Introduction

Desserts are the star of most meals, the much-appreciated sweetness that follows a savory course. Desserts can please the fussiest of tastes, as the variety is enormous. Despite often utilizing the same basic ingredients—eggs, butter, flour and milk—desserts come in hundreds of different shapes and sizes: the only limitations are the imagination and budget of the cook.

Chocolate and coffee are two delicious flavors for desserts. It's hard to believe that the chocolate cake was not the staple it is now a mere couple of centuries ago, as the cost of chocolate was too high for anybody but the very rich to afford. Coffee has only been a favorite flavor since 1650, when the first European coffee houses opened. And it was only in that same century that the first cakes, made with beaten eggs, became popular.

Pies, especially fruit pies in all their many forms, have long been a winning winter warmer. The natural sweetness of firm ripe peaches, pears and apples make them a sure hit for dessert, whether wrapped in pastry or submerged in a sweet syrup. The citrus fruits lend their tart, fresh flavor to cleanse the palate and add some zing to many desserts. And berries are a special treat with cream and cake or cookies.

When a little indulgence is called for—and desserts are synonymous with indulgence—you can't go past the comfort of a creamy pudding. Cheesecake, a crème brûlée or even an old-fashioned trifle are all classics that deserve to be discovered afresh.

No dessert book would be complete without a section on nut recipes. Whether coated with caramel or used ground or toasted in a cake or pie, nuts are a consistent crowd pleaser.

Like each volume in the *Little Guides* series, the recipes are presented in an easy-to-follow format suitable for cooks of all skill levels. Part 1—the basics section—provides you with the foundational recipes needed to create your favorite desserts, as well as hints on how to melt chocolate and roast nuts.

Part 2 is divided into four sections, covering chocolate and coffee; fruit; cream, cheese and milk; and nuts and coconut. That way you can head straight for your favorite flavor to browse for a suitable recipe. Feature pages scattered throughout highlight various special ingredients, and there is a glossary which not only explains, but also covers the uses and storage life of common items. Enjoy!

> *U.S. cup measures are used throughout this book. Slight adjustments may need to be made to quantities if Imperial or Metric cups are used.*

THE BASICS

In this handy section you'll learn all you need to know about preparing and baking pastry, melting chocolate and roasting nuts. With illustrated steps to guide you, dessert-making will be easier than ever before.

Basic Pie Pastry (Shortcrust)

PASTRY FOR
SINGLE-CRUST PIE

1¼ cups (6½ oz/195 g)
all-purpose (plain) flour

¼ teaspoon salt

⅓ cup (3 oz/90 g) vegetable
shortening or cold butter

3–4 tablespoons water

PASTRY FOR
DOUBLE-CRUST PIE

2 cups (10 oz/300 g)
all-purpose (plain) flour

½ teaspoon salt

⅔ cup (5 oz/150 g) vegetable
shortening or cold butter

6–7 tablespoons water

For the single-crust pastry, in a bowl, stir together flour and salt. Cut in the vegetable shortening or butter until pieces are the size of small peas. Sprinkle 1 tablespoon of the water over part of the mixture and gently toss with a fork. Push to the side of the bowl. Repeat until all the flour is moistened (you may not need all of the water). Form the dough into a ball. (If desired, chill for 1–24 hours.)

On a lightly floured work surface, flatten the dough with your hands. Roll the dough from the center to the edges, forming a circle about 12 inches (30 cm) in diameter (or as indicated).

Wrap pastry around rolling pin. Unroll onto a 9-inch (23-cm) pie plate (or as indicated). Or, fold pastry into quarters and place in pie plate; unfold. Ease the pastry into the pie plate, being careful not to stretch the pastry. Trim to ½ inch (1 cm) beyond the edge of the pie plate and fold the extra pastry under. Crimp the edge, if desired, and bake as directed.

For the double-crust pastry, prepare the dough as directed above, except divide in half. Form each half into a ball. (If desired, chill for 1–24 hours.) On a lightly floured surface, flatten one ball of dough with your hands. Roll the dough from the center to the edges, forming a circle about 12 inches (30 cm) in diameter (or as indicated).

Wrap pastry around rolling pin. Unroll onto a 9-inch (23-cm) pie plate (or as indicated). Or, fold pastry into quarters and place in pie plate; unfold. Ease pastry into the pie plate, being careful not to stretch pastry. Fill with desired filling. Trim pastry even with rim of pie plate.

For the top crust, roll remaining dough. Cut slits to allow steam to escape. Place the top crust on the filling. Trim the top crust ½ inch (1 cm) beyond the edge

of the plate. Fold the top crust under the bottom crust; crimp edge or press together with the tines of a fork. Bake as directed.

To prepare pastry in a food processor, add flour, salt and vegetable shortening or butter. Process with on/off turns until most of the mixture resembles cornmeal but a few larger pieces remain. With machine running, quickly add 3 tablespoons water for a single-crust pie, or ¼ cup (2 fl oz/60 ml) cold water for a double-crust pie, through the feed tube. Stop the processor as soon as all the water is added. Scrape down sides. Process with 2 on/off turns (the mixture may

not all be moistened). Remove from bowl and shape into 1 or 2 equal balls. (If desired, chill for 1–24 hours.) Continue as above.

For a fully baked pastry shell, prepare as above, except prick the bottom and sides of the crust generously with the tines of a fork. Prick where the bottom and sides meet all around crust. Line pastry shell with a double thickness of aluminum foil.

Bake in a preheated 450°F (220°C/Gas Mark 6) oven for 8 minutes. Remove the foil and bake for 5–6 minutes more or until golden brown. Cool on a rack. Fill as directed in recipe.

don't use your
fingers to blend
a dough made
with shortening
because it will
be too sticky
to handle

STEP 1

Cutting in Shortening or Butter

With a pastry blender, a fork or two knives, cut in the
shortening or butter until the pieces are the size of small
peas. Use a light touch; if the mixture is overworked,
the crust won't be flaky.

be sure the water
is very cold; if the
water from your
tap isn't cold
enough, add ice

STEP 2

Incorporating Water

Sprinkle water, 1 tablespoon at a time, over part of the
flour and shortening or butter mixture, while gently
tossing with a fork to combine. Push moistened dough
to one side of the bowl; repeat until all the dough is
moistened (you may not need to use all of the water).

to pick up
any crumbs, push
the ball of dough
against the bottom
and sides of
the bowl

STEP 3

Forming into a Ball

After the shortening or butter, water and dry ingredients
are combined, gather the dough into a ball by scooping
up and compressing the mixture with your hands or by
pulling it together with a fork.

always roll from
the center just to
the edge of the
dough without
going off the sides
of the pastry

STEP 4

Rolling Dough

Dust the surface with more flour, if needed, and rub
the rolling pin with flour. With a light, fluid movement,
roll from the center of the dough out to the edge. Move
the rolling pin around the dough to make a circle that is
uniformly thick and well-shaped, or roll the dough, give
it a quarter turn, then roll again. Repeat this action until
the dough is of the desired thickness.

if necessary, brush
excess flour from
the dough with
a pastry brush

STEP 5

Transferring the Dough

Loosely drape the dough around the rolling pin and lay
it across the pie plate. Unroll and gently ease the dough
into the plate without stretching it.

hold the pan
steady with
one hand when
piercing the crust
with a fork

STEP 6

Fully Baking a Crust

When a crust needs to be fully baked before filling, it
must first be pricked all over so that the steam built up
during cooking can escape. Then line the crust with a
double thickness of aluminum foil.

Tart Pastry

1¼ cups (6½ oz/195 g)
all-purpose (plain) flour

¼ cup (2 oz/60 g) sugar

½ cup (4 oz/120 g) cold butter

2 egg yolks, beaten

1 tablespoon chilled water

In a bowl, stir together the flour and sugar. Cut in butter until pieces are the size of small peas. In a small bowl, stir together the egg yolks and water. Gradually stir the egg yolk mixture into the flour mixture. Gently knead the dough just until a ball forms.

To prepare in a food processor, add the flour, sugar and butter.

Process with on/off turns until pieces are the size of small peas. Stir together the egg yolks and water. With machine running, quickly add the liquid through the feed tube. Stop the machine as soon as all the liquid is added. Process with 2 more on/off turns.

Remove the dough and shape into a ball. For easier handling, cover dough with plastic wrap and chill for 30–60 minutes. Use as directed in the recipe you are making or proceed as follows.

Roll out the dough on a lightly floured work surface to a circle 2 inches (5 cm) larger than the diameter of the tart pan. To make

sure that the dough circle is the correct size, lay the pan on the dough and measure the margin with a ruler.

Transfer the dough from the work surface to the pan as for a single-crust pie. With one hand, lift up a section of overhanging dough and ease it into the pan (see Step 1) so it fits snugly, especially where the bottom and sides meet.

Let some dough hang over the side of the tart pan all the way around. Be sure that the dough is fitted into the tart pan before trimming, or the pie crust will shrink when baked.

TART PASTRY

To remove excess dough, roll around the entire edge of the tart pan with a rolling pin (see Step 2). The overhanging dough will drop off, leaving a neat edge. Instead of using a rolling pin, you can use your thumb to trim away the extra dough (see Step 3).

When done, remove the baked tart from the oven and let cool slightly. Set on a lidded jar, a metal can or any other heatproof sturdy container. The sides of the tart pan will fall away. Then carefully transfer the tart to a wire rack to cool completely (leave the pan bottom in place) before serving.

STEPS FOR MAKING TART PASTRY

you can also fit the dough into the pan with your fingers or the heel of your hand, rather than a ball of dough

STEP I

Fitting the Dough in the Tart Pan
Transfer the dough from the work surface to the pan. With one hand, lift up a section of the overhanging dough and ease it into the pan. Use a small ball of dough to push against the inside of the dough so it fits snugly, especially where the bottom and sides meet.

STEPS FOR MAKING TART PASTRY

be sure that the dough is fitted into the pan before trimming or the crust will shrink when baked

STEP 2

Trimming Pastry with a Rolling Pin
To remove the excess dough, roll around the edge of the pan with a rolling pin. Use an even, smooth action. The overhanging dough will drop off, leaving a neat edge.

push from the outside in so that the inside edge of the pan is fully covered with dough

STEP 3

Trimming Pastry with your Fingers
Instead of using a rolling pin, you can use your thumb to trim away the extra dough. Lift up the dough with one hand and push across the rim of the tart pan with the thumb of your other hand.

The Basics

Sweet Pastry Dough (Pâte Sucrée)

½ cup (4 oz/120 g), plus
1 tablespoon, unsalted butter
at room temperature, cut
into pieces

½ cup (2 oz/60 g)
confectioners' (icing) sugar,
sifted

1 egg

2 cups (10 oz/300 g)
all-purpose (plain) flour

⅛ teaspoon baking powder

In a bowl, combine the butter
and sugar. Using an electric
mixer on low speed, beat until
smooth, about 3 minutes.

Add the egg and beat until
creamy. Using a rubber spatula,
fold in the flour and baking
powder just until incorporated.
Then beat with the electric
mixer on low speed until the
dough is evenly mixed and
clings together, 2–3 minutes.

Shape the dough into a ball,
wrap tightly in plastic wrap and
refrigerate for at least 2 hours
or as long as 2 weeks. Bring
to room temperature before
using, then use as directed in
the recipe you are following.

Quick Puff Pastry

————◆◆◆————

4 cups (1¼ lb/600 g)
all-purpose (plain) flour

1 teaspoon salt

2 cups (1 lb/480 g) cold butter

1¼ cups (10 fl oz/300 ml)
ice water

In a large bowl, stir together the flour and the salt. Cut the cold butter into ½-inch-thick (1-cm-thick) slices (not cubes). Add the butter slices to the flour mixture; using a spoon, toss until the butter slices are coated with the flour mixture and are separated. (Do not toss with your hands, as your body heat will soften the butter pieces.)

Pour ice water over the flour mixture. Using a spoon, quickly mix. (The butter will remain in large pieces and the flour will not be completely moistened.)

Turn dough out onto a lightly floured surface. Knead dough 10 times, pressing and pushing dough together to form a rough-looking ball. Shape dough into a rectangle (the dough still will have some dry-looking areas). Make the corners as square as possible. Slightly flatten dough.

Working on a well-floured work surface, roll the dough into an 18- x 15-inch (45- x 38-cm) rectangle. Always roll from the center out, stopping short of the dough edges so the layers are not pinched together. The dough will still look somewhat rough; it becomes smoother with repeated rolling.

Next, make a letter-fold: working crosswise, fold one-third of the dough to the center, then another third over it to form a 15- x 6-inch (38- x 15-cm) rectangle. Give the dough a quarter turn.

Fold crosswise into thirds again to form a 5- x 6-inch (13- x 15-cm) rectangle. By folding, turning and folding again, the dough is now in 9 layers.

QUICK PUFF PASTRY

Repeat the rolling, folding, turning and folding process once more, forming a 5- x 4-inch (13- x 10-cm) rectangle. Wrap the dough with plastic wrap and chill for 20 minutes. Repeat the rolling and folding process 2 more times.

Before using, chill the dough for another 20 minutes. To use the dough in a recipe, cut it in half crosswise. Each half will make a 1⅓-lb (660 g) portion.

STEPS FOR FOLDING QUICK PUFF PASTRY

generously flour the work surface so the dough doesn't adhere

STEP 1

Folding into Thirds

Make a letter-fold: working crosswise, fold one-third of the dough to the center, then another third over it to form a 15- x 6-inch (38- x 15-cm) rectangle. Give the dough a quarter turn.

the dough will look somewhat rough but it gets smoother with repeated rolling

STEP 2

Folding Again

Fold the dough crosswise into thirds again to form a 5- x 6-inch (13- x 15-cm) rectangle. By folding, turning and folding again, the dough is now in 9 layers.

always roll from the center out, stopping short of the edges so the layers are not pinched together

STEP 3

Rolling the Dough Again

Roll, fold, turn and fold one more time. The dough will now be a 5- x 4-inch (13- x 10-cm) rectangle. Wrap with plastic wrap and chill for 20 minutes. Repeat the process 2 more times.

Cream Puff Pastry

½ cup (4 oz/120 g) butter

1 cup (8 fl oz/240 ml) water

¼ teaspoon salt

1 cup (5 oz/150 g)
all-purpose (plain) flour

4 eggs

Preheat an oven to 400°F (200°C/Gas Mark 5) and lightly butter a baking sheet.

Place the butter in a medium saucepan. Add water and salt. Bring to a boil, stirring until the butter melts. Add the flour all at once, stirring vigorously. Cook and stir until the mixture forms a ball that doesn't separate and that pulls away from the side of the pan. Remove from the heat and cool for 10 minutes. (This ensures that the eggs will not curdle when they are added.)

Add the eggs, one at a time, to the flour mixture, beating with a wooden spoon after each for 1–2 minutes, or until smooth. The mixture will look lumpy at first, but it will become thick, shiny and silky.

Use as directed in the recipe you are following, or proceed as follows for cream puffs or éclairs.

Shape the cream puffs (see Step 1) on the baking sheet.

Bake for about 30 minutes, or until golden brown. Remove puffs from sheet. Cool on a rack.

To hollow out the puffs so that they can be filled, slice off the tops (or cut in half). With a fork, gently scrape out any soft, moist dough. Work carefully so that you don't puncture the crust.

Fill the shells just before serving so they don't become soggy. If you make the shells in advance, store them in an airtight container overnight before filling.

Shape the éclairs (see Step 2) on the prepared baking sheet and bake for about 30 minutes, or until golden brown. Cool.

The Basics

you can also use
a rubber spatula
to push the dough
off the spoon

STEP 1

Shaping Cream Puffs

Scoop up some dough with a tablespoon. Use another spoon to push off the dough in a mound onto the baking sheet. Leave 3 inches (7.5 cm) between the puffs as they will expand as they cook.

squeeze out
the dough with
a gentle, even
pressure

STEP 2

Piping Eclairs

Fit a pastry (piping) bag with a ½-inch (1-cm) plain tip. Pipe strips of dough 3 inches (7.5 cm) apart onto a greased baking sheet. Cut off the dough with a knife at the tip for a neat finish.

Génoise

½ cup (4 oz/120 g) sugar

4 eggs

¾ cup (4 oz/120 g) all-purpose (plain) flour

Preheat an oven to 400°F (200°C/Gas Mark 5). Butter and flour a 10-inch (25-cm) round cake pan.

In a large heatproof bowl, combine the sugar and eggs. Place over (not touching) gently simmering water in a pan. Whisk until the mixture feels lukewarm, then remove from the pan and, using an electric mixer on high speed

or a wire whisk, beat until cool and the batter falls in a thick ribbon that holds its shape for 3–4 seconds, about 15 minutes. Sift the flour over the batter and, using a rubber spatula, fold it in. Pour into the prepared pan and smooth the top.

Bake just until the cake springs back to the touch, 20 minutes. Invert onto a rack, carefully lift off the pan and allow to cool completely. Cut into layers if desired, or as directed in the recipe you are following.

Pastry Cream

2¼ cups (18 fl oz/540 ml) milk

½ cup (4 fl oz/120 ml) heavy (double) cream

¾ cup (6 oz/180 g) sugar

5 tablespoons (1½ oz/45 g) cornstarch (cornflour)

1 whole egg, plus 1 egg yolk

1 teaspoon vanilla extract (essence)

In a heavy saucepan over medium heat, combine 1½ cups (12 fl oz/360 ml) of the milk, the cream and sugar and bring almost to a boil, whisking once or twice to dissolve the sugar.

Meanwhile, place the cornstarch in a small bowl and add ½ cup (4 fl oz/120 ml) of the milk, stirring to dissolve the cornstarch. Add the remaining milk, the whole egg, egg yolk and vanilla. Whisk together until smooth.

When the hot milk mixture is about to boil, pour in the cornstarch mixture, whisking continuously until completely blended. Continue to heat the mixture, whisking constantly, until it boils and thickens to the consistency of custard pudding. Remove from the heat, pour into a bowl and press a piece of plastic wrap directly onto the surface to prevent a skin forming. Let cool completely before using or refrigerating. Refrigerate for up to 1 week before use.

Makes 3 cups (24 fl oz/720 ml)

Crème Anglaise

1 cup (8 fl oz/240 ml) milk

1 vanilla bean, split lengthwise

4 egg yolks, at room temperature

½ cup (2 oz/60 g) sugar

In a saucepan, combine the milk and vanilla bean and bring to a boil. Meanwhile, in a large bowl, whisk together the egg yolks and sugar. As soon as the milk boils, remove from the heat. Remove the vanilla bean and, using a knife tip, scrape the seeds into the milk; discard the bean.

Pour half of the boiling milk into the bowl holding the egg mixture, whisking vigorously. Return the pan to the heat, bring the milk to a boil and pour the egg mixture into the pan, whisking continuously.

Stir over medium heat until the custard lightly coats the back of a wooden spoon, 2–3 minutes. You should have about 1 cup (8 fl oz/240 ml).

Remove from the heat. Press plastic wrap directly onto the surface to prevent a skin from forming and allow to cool.

Makes about 1 cup (8 fl oz/240 ml)

Sugar-roasted Almonds

4 teaspoons granulated sugar

¼ cup (2 fl oz/60 ml) water

1 cup (4½ oz/135 g) slivered blanched almonds

Preheat an oven to 350°F (180°C/Gas Mark 4).

In a small saucepan, combine the granulated sugar and water and bring to a boil, stirring to dissolve the sugar. Remove the syrup from the heat.

Spread the almonds on a baking sheet. Drizzle with the sugar and water syrup and stir well to coat the almonds.

Roast, stirring every 5 minutes, until the almonds are a pale golden brown, about 5 minutes. Let cool, then use immediately or store in an airtight container for up to 4 weeks.

Makes 1 cup (4½ oz/135 g)

Using and Melting Chocolate

Great care should be taken when melting chocolate. It burns very easily and this makes the flavor bitter. If overheated, it becomes hard and granular.

Be careful not to let even the slightest amount of steam or water come into contact with the chocolate, or it will "seize" (stiffen and solidify). Nothing can be done once this has happened; you will have to throw the chocolate out and start again. This problem does not arise if a recipe calls for chocolate to be combined with butter or vegetable shortening and then melted.

To melt chocolate on its own on the stovetop, use a double boiler or a heatproof bowl that fits snugly over a saucepan. Put a small amount of cold water in the bottom part of the boiler or in the saucepan; do not allow the water to touch the bottom of the bowl or top boiler. Bring the water to a gentle simmer and then remove from the heat. Place the chocolate in the bowl or top boiler and return the saucepan to the heat, if necessary, stirring to melt the chocolate. Do not cover the bowl; this will cause steam to condense on the cover and fall into the chocolate and it will "seize."

Chocolate that is to be melted with butter or shortening may be placed in a heavy-bottomed saucepan on the stovetop over a low heat. Cook, stirring often, until melted and smooth, then immediately remove from the heat and use as directed.

The dry heat of the microwave oven is perfect for melting chocolate. Place the chocolate pieces (and butter or shortening, if using) in a heatproof glass dish and microwave on high for 1–3 minutes, stirring 1–2 times during melting depending on the amount to be melted. The chocolate will retain its shape, so stir it to melt it fully.

Another method uses a heavy-duty plastic bag. Put the chocolate (and butter or shortening, if using) in the bag and push the contents to one corner. Tie the bag just above the mixture, then set the bag in a bowl of warm water to melt. Rub the bag to blend the contents. This method is useful when decorating cakes, as you can just snip a tiny piece from the corner of the bag to create an icing bag with which you can drizzle the chocolate over your dessert.

MELTING CHOCOLATE

the chocolate will melt more quickly if first broken or chopped into small pieces

Place the chocolate pieces and shortening or butter (if called for) in the top of a double-boiler or in a heatproof bowl set over (not touching) simmering water in a pan. Do not cover. Cook over low heat, stirring often, until melted and smooth.

DESSERT RECIPES

Desserts can take any form to suit your fancy. Cakes,
pies, puddings and profiteroles—all can be equally
tempting in their own way. Browse through the
recipes, then cook, eat and enjoy.

CHOCOLATE AND COFFEE

Warm Chocolate Cake

18 oz (540 g) bittersweet (plain) chocolate, chopped

¾ cup (6 oz/180 g) unsalted butter, cut into pieces

4 eggs

3 tablespoons granulated sugar

½ cup (2 oz/60 g) cake (soft-wheat) flour, sifted

Confectioners' (icing) sugar

Unsweetened cocoa powder

Preheat an oven to 350°F (180°C/Gas Mark 4). Butter a 9-inch (23-cm) round cake pan.

In the top pan of a double boiler or a heatproof bowl set over (not touching) simmering water in a pan, combine the chocolate and butter and stir until melted and smooth. Remove from the heat.

Put the eggs and granulated sugar together in a stainless steel bowl and place over the lower pan of simmering water. Whisk vigorously until well combined, about 4 minutes. Remove from the heat. Using an electric mixer, beat on high speed until the mixture is pale yellow and falls in thick ribbons when the beaters are lifted, 5–10 minutes.

Reduce the speed to low, add the melted chocolate mixture and beat until blended. Stop to scrape down the sides of the bowl, then beat on low speed until smooth. Add the flour and beat until smooth; do not overmix. Pour the batter into the prepared cake pan and place on a baking sheet. Bake for 15 minutes.

Remove from the oven and run a sharp knife around the sides of the pan to loosen the cake. Invert onto a plate, lift off the pan and invert again onto a serving platter. Sift a heavy coating of confectioners' sugar over the top, then lightly dust with the cocoa. Cut into thin slices and serve immediately.

NOTE The cake can be made up to 1 day in advance and reheated in a preheated 350°F (180°C/Gas Mark 4) oven for 4 minutes.

Serves 8

Fudge Brownies

4 oz (120 g) unsweetened (bitter) chocolate, chopped

¾ cup (6 oz/180 g) unsalted butter, cut into pieces

4 eggs

2 cups (1 lb/480 g) granulated sugar

1 teaspoon vanilla extract (essence)

1 cup (5 oz/150 g) all-purpose (plain) flour

½ teaspoon baking powder

½ teaspoon salt

1 cup (5 oz/150 g) roughly chopped almonds

1 tablespoon confectioners' (icing) sugar

Preheat an oven to 350°F (180°C/Gas Mark 4). Butter a 9- x 13-inch (23- x 33-cm) baking pan.

In the top pan of a double boiler or in a heatproof bowl set over (not touching) simmering water in a pan, combine the chocolate and butter and stir until melted and smooth. Remove from the heat and let cool.

In a bowl, using an electric mixer on medium speed, beat together the eggs and granulated sugar until the mixture is pale yellow and falls in thick ribbons when the beaters are lifted, 3–4 minutes.

Stir in the vanilla and the cooled chocolate-butter mixture until no streaks remain; do not overmix. Using a spatula, fold in the flour, baking powder and salt until just blended. Fold in the almonds.

Pour the batter into the baking pan. Bake until a wooden skewer inserted into the center comes out with a few crumbs attached, 25–30 minutes.

Transfer to a rack and let cool in the pan. Cut into 2-inch (5-cm) squares. Just before serving, using a fine-mesh sieve or sifter, dust lightly with the confectioners' sugar.

Makes 24

Mocha Zabaglione

8 egg yolks

½ cup (4 oz/120 g) sugar

2 tablespoons unsweetened cocoa powder, plus extra for dusting

¼ cup (2 fl oz/60 ml) Marsala

¼ cup (2 fl oz/60 ml) coffee liqueur

½ cup (4 fl oz/120 ml) sweet white wine

Fresh fruit or sponge finger cookies (savoiardi/ladyfingers) (optional), to serve

In the top pan of a double boiler or in a heatproof bowl set over (not touching) simmering water in a pan, place the egg yolks, the sugar and the cocoa. Using an electric mixer on medium to high speed, beat until combined.

Add the Marsala and coffee liqueur and beat until combined and creamy. Add the wine and continue to beat for about 10 minutes, or until thick and creamy. Remove from the heat and stir vigorously with a wooden spoon.

Pour into six glasses and dust with the additional cocoa. Serve with fresh fruit or sponge finger cookies, if desired.

Makes 6

Chocolate Bundt Cake

CAKE

1 cup (8 oz/240 g) butter, softened

1 cup (7 oz/210 g) superfine (caster) sugar

4 medium eggs, beaten

1¼ cups (5 oz/150 g) self-rising flour

½ cup (1½ oz/45 g) unsweetened cocoa powder

TOPPING

5 oz (150 g) bittersweet (plain) or semisweet (plain) chocolate

3 tablespoons unsalted butter

Maraschino cherries (optional), to serve

Preheat an oven to 350°F (180°C/Gas Mark 4). Grease a 9-inch (23-cm) ring or bundt pan and line the bottom with parchment (baking) paper.

For the cake, cream the butter and sugar until very light and smooth. Slowly incorporate the eggs, then fold in the flour and the cocoa, mixing until thoroughly combined. Spoon into the prepared cake pan.

Bake for about 50 minutes, or until a wooden skewer inserted into the center of the cake comes out clean.

Cool in the pan for a few minutes, then turn out onto a wire rack to cool.

For the topping, in a double boiler or in a heatproof bowl set over (not touching) simmering water in a pan, slowly melt the chocolate. Stir in the butter. Pour over the top of the cake, allowing it to flow down the sides. Decorate with cherries, if desired.

Serves 8

Chocolate Terrine with Raspberry Sauce

CHOCOLATE TERRINE

13 oz (390 g) bittersweet (plain) chocolate, chopped

½ cup (4 oz/120 g) butter, at room temperature

4 egg yolks

2½ oz (75 g) confectioners' (icing) sugar

½ teaspoon ground cinnamon

2 cups (16 fl oz/480 ml) heavy (double) cream

2–3 drops vanilla extract (essence)

RASPBERRY SAUCE

1 cup (4 oz/120 g) raspberries

3–4 tablespoons confectioners' (icing) sugar, or to taste, sifted

1 tablespoon orange juice, Cointreau or other liqueur

Whole raspberries (optional), to serve

For the chocolate terrine, melt the chocolate and butter in the top of a double boiler or in a heatproof bowl set over (not touching) simmering water in a pan. Remove from the heat.

In a large bowl, using an electric mixer on medium to high speed, beat the egg yolks with the confectioners' sugar and the cinnamon until foamy. Add the chocolate mixture and beat until combined. Set aside to cool.

Whip the cream, add the vanilla and continue to whip until the cream forms peaks. Gently fold it into the chocolate batter.

Line an 11-inch (28-cm) cake mold with parchment (baking) or waxed (greaseproof) paper and pour in the batter. Cover and refrigerate for 12–24 hours.

For the raspberry sauce, in a food processor, purée the raspberries. Pass through a fine-mesh sieve into a bowl; discard the contents of the sieve. Stir in the sugar and the orange juice or liqueur. Chill before serving.

To serve, unmold the cake and serve it sliced, with the sauce. Sprinkle with the raspberries, if desired.

Serves 12

Chocolate Cream Puffs

PASTRY PUFFS

1 cup (8 fl oz/240 ml) water

2½ oz (75 g) unsalted butter, cut into small pieces

¼ teaspoon salt

½ teaspoon sugar

¾ cup (4 oz/120 g) all-purpose (plain) flour, sifted

5 eggs

CHOCOLATE CREAM

13 oz (390 g) semisweet (plain) chocolate, finely chopped

2 cups (16 fl oz/480 ml) heavy (double) cream

¼ cup (2 oz/60 g) sugar

Preheat an oven to 400°F (200°C/Gas Mark 5). Butter and flour a large baking sheet.

For the pastry puffs, in a saucepan, combine the water, butter, salt and the ½ teaspoon sugar and bring to a boil. As soon as it boils, remove the pan from the heat and add the flour all at once. Using a rubber spatula or a wooden spoon, briskly beat in the flour. Place the saucepan over high heat and continue beating for 2 minutes. Remove from the heat again and scrape the contents of the pan into a bowl.

Add 4 of the eggs, one at a time, beating vigorously after each addition until smooth.

CHOCOLATE CREAM PUFFS

Place the dough in a pastry (piping) bag with a ½-inch (1-cm) plain tip. Pipe mounds 2 inches (5 cm) in diameter and 3 inches (7.5 cm) apart onto the baking sheet. You should have 16–20 mounds.

In a bowl, beat the remaining egg until well blended. Using a pastry brush, lightly brush each mound with the beaten egg.

Bake until the puffs are golden brown, about 30 minutes. Transfer the puffs to a rack and let cool completely, about 30 minutes.

When the puffs are cool, slice off the top one-third of each puff. Reserve the tops.

For the chocolate cream, place the chocolate in the top pan of a double boiler or in a heatproof bowl set over (not touching) simmering water in a pan. Stir just until the chocolate melts, then remove from the heat.

Pour the cream into a bowl. Using an electric mixer set on high speed, beat until soft peaks form. Add the ¼ cup (2 oz/ 60 g) sugar and beat until stiff peaks form, about 20 seconds.

Pour all of the melted chocolate into the whipped cream as quickly as possible, and mix on high speed until combined, about 1 minute.

Place the chocolate cream in a clean pastry (piping) bag fitted with a ½-inch (1-cm) plain tip. Pipe the cream into the bottoms of the cooled puffs so a little bit of the cream is exposed between the crusts. Replace the tops on the filled bottoms and serve immediately.

Makes 16 to 20

Chocolate Soufflé

◆━◆◆◆━◆

¼ cup (2 oz/60 g) unsalted butter, melted

2 tablespoons plus ½ cup (4 oz/120 g) granulated sugar

3 oz (90 g) unsweetened (bitter) chocolate, finely chopped

3 egg yolks

5 egg whites

Confectioners' (icing) sugar (optional), to serve

Preheat an oven to 375°F (190°C/Gas Mark 4). Brush the melted butter on the bottom and sides of a soufflé dish 8 inches (20 cm) in diameter and 4 inches (10 cm) deep.

Place the prepared soufflé dish in a refrigerator for about 2 minutes, then sprinkle the bottom and sides with the 2 tablespoons granulated sugar, coating evenly.

Place the chocolate in the top pan of a double boiler or in a heatproof bowl set over (not touching) simmering water in a pan. Stir just until the chocolate melts, then remove it from the heat. Add ¼ cup (2 oz/60 g) of the remaining granulated sugar, stir to combine, then whisk in the egg yolks. Remove from the heat and let cool.

Place the egg whites in a clean bowl and, using an electric mixer set on medium-high speed, beat the egg whites until they form soft peaks. Add the remaining ¼ cup (2 oz/60 g) granulated sugar and beat until stiff peaks form.

Using a rubber spatula and working in several batches, carefully fold the egg whites into the melted chocolate until no streaks remain. Do not overmix. Pour the mixture into the soufflé dish.

Bake until the top of the soufflé has risen and is firm to the touch, 20–25 minutes. Sift the confectioners' sugar lightly over the top, if desired, then serve immediately.

Serves 4 to 6

Coffee and Armagnac Parfait

⅔ cup (5 oz/150 g) sugar

⅓ cup (3 fl oz/90 ml) water

4 egg yolks

2 cups (16 fl oz/480 ml) heavy (double) cream

2½ tablespoons coffee extract (essence)

⅓ cup (3 fl oz/90 ml) Armagnac

Unsweetened cocoa powder

In a saucepan, combine the sugar and water. Stir until the sugar is dissolved; bring to a boil over high heat.

Meanwhile, place the egg yolks in a heatproof bowl. As soon as the sugar-water syrup boils, remove from the heat and slowly pour the mixture into the egg yolks while whisking vigorously.

Place the bowl over (not touching) simmering water in a pan. Continue to whisk vigorously until the mixture is frothy and stiff, 3–4 minutes.

Remove the bowl from over the water and, using an electric mixer on high speed or the whisk, continue to beat until the mixture cools down completely, about 5 minutes. Set aside.

Place the cream in a large bowl. Using an electric mixer fitted with clean beaters, beat until soft peaks form. Add the coffee extract, Armagnac and cooled yolk mixture and, using a spatula, fold together gently.

Divide the mixture evenly among 4–6 individual parfait glasses. Cover and freeze for at least 5 hours or, preferably, overnight.

Serve each parfait garnished with a dusting of cocoa, if desired.

Makes 4 to 6

About Coffee

Coffee probably originated in Ethiopia, Africa, where small coffee trees still grow in a semi-wild state. In the sixteenth century, coffee arrived in Egypt and it was not long before the practice of coffee drinking spread to the western European nations. Of the many species of coffee plants, the most important is *Coffea arabica*, which grows only at high altitudes. It is from this species that premium coffees are produced. Most ordinary coffee comes from *C. canephora*, which grows at lower altitudes and is more widely cultivated, often for use in blended coffees.

After harvesting, the red, cherry-sized fruits of the plants are allowed to ferment, then the pulp and skins are removed. At this stage, the beans are grey-green to yellow-brown and have no trace of coffee flavor; the flavor develops when the beans are roasted. This specialized process, which differs from one producer to another, is possibly the most important step in coffee production. Coffees are usually labeled with their origin, for example Jamaica or Kenya, and their roast, which may be light, medium or dark.

Coffee beans begin to lose their flavorsome essential oils as soon as they are roasted; the rate of loss accelerates rapidly once the beans are ground. For this reason, coffee is best bought as whole beans, in small quantities, and ground only as needed. Store beans in an airtight container in a cool cupboard for up to 2 weeks or in the refrigerator for up to 1 month. For longer or bulk storage, wrap them well in plastic and freeze for up to 3 months.

Chocolate Puddings
with Raspberry Sauce

RASPBERRY SAUCE

1½ cups (6 oz/180 g) raspberries

3 tablespoons confectioners' (icing) sugar, or to taste

CHOCOLATE PUDDINGS

3 teaspoons plus ¼ cup (2 oz/60 g) granulated sugar

3 oz (90 g) bittersweet (plain) chocolate

5 tablespoons (2½ oz/75 g) unsalted butter

3 extra-large egg yolks

2 extra-large egg whites

¼ cup (1½ oz/45 g) all-purpose (plain) flour, sifted

1 small block white chocolate, for chocolate curls

Whole raspberries (optional), to serve

For the raspberry sauce, in a food processor, purée the raspberries. Pass the purée through a fine-mesh sieve into a bowl; discard the contents of the sieve. Stir in the confectioners' sugar until well combined and the sugar has dissolved.

Preheat an oven to 425°F (210°C/Gas Mark 5). Butter 4 standard-sized (½-cup/ 4-fl oz/120-ml) muffin pans, then sprinkle the bottom and sides with 2 teaspoons of the granulated sugar.

For the chocolate puddings, combine the bittersweet chocolate and butter in the top pan of a double boiler or in a heatproof bowl set over (not touching) simmering water in a pan. Stir until the chocolate melts, then remove from the heat and let cool slightly.

Meanwhile, in a bowl, using an electric mixer on high speed, beat together the egg yolks and the ¼ cup (2 oz/60 g) of granulated sugar until thick and creamy. Reduce the mixer speed to medium and slowly pour in the melted chocolate.

In a clean bowl, using clean beaters, beat the egg whites until very soft peaks form. Sprinkle in the remaining 1 teaspoon granulated sugar and continue to beat until soft peaks form.

Using a rubber spatula or a whisk, fold the flour into the chocolate batter alternately with the egg whites, beginning and ending with the flour.

Pour the batter into the molds, filling to within ⅛ inch (3 mm) of the rims.

Place the pan in the center of the oven and immediately reduce the temperature to 375°F (190°C/Gas Mark 4). Bake until puffy and a thin but firm crust forms on top, 15 minutes. Do not open the oven door during the first 6 minutes of baking. Transfer the pan to a wire rack and let rest for 4–5 minutes to ease unmolding.

Meanwhile, run a vegetable peeler along the block of white chocolate to form curls. Keep the curls cool until serving.

Run a sharp knife around the edge of each cup and quickly invert the puddings onto the rack. Transfer the puddings to individual plates, top-sides facing down.

Pour the raspberry sauce evenly around the puddings and then sprinkle with the white chocolate curls. Scatter fresh raspberries around each pudding, if desired. Serve immediately.

Makes 4

Chocolate and Raspberry Napoleons

Quick Puff Pastry (page 21)

CHOCOLATE PASTRY CREAM

¼ cup (2 oz/60 g) granulated sugar

2 tablespoons all-purpose (plain) flour

⅛ teaspoon salt

1 cup (8 fl oz/240 ml) light (single) cream

1 oz (30 g) semisweet (plain) chocolate, chopped

2 slightly beaten egg yolks

½ teaspoon vanilla extract (essence)

¼ cup (2 fl oz/60 ml) whipping cream

GLAZE

2 cups (8 oz/240 g) confectioners' (icing) sugar

¼ teaspoon vanilla extract (essence)

2–3 tablespoons boiling water

⅓ cup (3½ oz/105 g) seedless raspberry preserves

1½ tablespoons melted semisweet (plain) chocolate

Preheat an oven to 425°F (210°C/Gas Mark 5). Line 2 baking sheets with parchment (baking) paper; set aside.

On a lightly floured surface, roll the dough into a 10-inch (25-cm) square. Using a sharp knife, trim off about ½ inch (1 cm) from all 4 sides to make a 9-inch (23-cm) square. Cut pastry into nine 3-inch (7.5-cm) squares. Transfer pastry squares to the baking sheets; prick pastry. Bake for 18–23 minutes, or until golden. Carefully remove pastries from baking sheets. Cool on a rack.

Meanwhile, for the chocolate pastry cream, in a heavy, medium saucepan stir together the granulated sugar, flour and salt. Slowly stir in the cream; add chocolate. Stir over medium heat until mixture is thickened and bubbly. Cook and stir for

1 minute more. Slowly stir about half of the hot mixture into beaten egg yolks. Return all to saucepan. Cook and stir for 2 minutes more. Remove from heat. Stir in vanilla. Transfer mixture to a bowl. Cover surface with plastic wrap and cool just until warm without stirring. In a small bowl, beat whipping cream until soft peaks form. Fold whipped cream into warm chocolate pastry cream.

For the glaze, in a medium bowl combine confectioners' sugar and vanilla. Stir in enough boiling water to make a glaze of spreading consistency; set aside. To assemble, use the tines of a fork to separate each pastry square horizontally into 3 layers. Spread 1 teaspoon of the raspberry preserves on

each bottom layer. Spread about 12 tablespoons of the pastry cream over raspberry preserves. Top with middle pastry layers. Spread another 12 tablespoons of the pastry cream on each middle layer. Finally, top with remaining pastry layers. Spread glaze

over top layer, then drizzle with melted chocolate. Chill up to 1 hour before serving.

Makes 9

59

Cappuccino Gelato

1½ cups (12 fl oz/360 ml) milk

½ cup (4 fl oz/120 ml) light (single) cream

¼ cup (2 oz/60 g) sugar

4 extra-large egg yolks

2 teaspoons vanilla extract (essence)

2 tablespoons instant coffee granules dissolved in 1 tablespoon milk or 3 tablespoons brewed coffee mixed with 1 tablespoon coffee liqueur

In a saucepan over medium heat, combine the milk, cream and sugar and stir to dissolve the sugar. Bring almost to a boil, then remove from the heat.

In a small bowl, stir together the egg yolks until blended. Stir a few tablespoons of the hot milk mixture into the egg yolks. Then slowly pour the egg yolks into the hot milk mixture, stirring constantly.

Place over low heat and cook, stirring, until thickened, about 2 minutes. Do not allow the mixture to boil. Immediately pour the mixture through a fine-mesh sieve into a bowl to remove any lumps. Stir in the vanilla and the coffee mixture. Let cool, cover and chill well, at least 2 hours.

Transfer the coffee mixture to an ice-cream maker. Freeze according to the manufacturer's instructions.

Serves 4

61

Mile-High Chocolate Layer Cake

CAKE

2¼ cups (11½ oz/345 g) all-purpose (plain) flour

1½ teaspoons baking soda (bicarbonate of soda)

1 teaspoon salt

1¼ teaspoons baking powder

4 oz (120 g) unsweetened (bitter) chocolate, chopped

¾ cup (6 oz/180 g) unsalted butter, at room temperature

1¾ cups (14 oz/420 g) sugar

3 eggs

1 teaspoon vanilla extract (essence)

¾ cup (6 fl oz/180 ml) milk

FROSTING

2 cups (16 fl oz/480 ml) heavy (double) cream

15 oz (450 g) semisweet (plain) chocolate, chopped

⅓ cup (3 oz/90 g) unsalted butter, at room temperature

1½ tablespoons vanilla extract (essence)

Preheat an oven to 350°F (180°C/Gas Mark 4). Butter and line three 9-inch (23-cm) round cake pans.

For the cake, in a large bowl, mix together the flour, baking soda, salt and baking powder.

In the top pan of a double boiler or in a heatproof bowl set over (not touching) simmering water in a pan, melt the chocolate, stirring until smooth. Remove from the heat and let cool to room temperature.

In a large bowl, using an electric mixer set on medium speed, beat together the butter and sugar until light and fluffy, 3–5 minutes. Add the eggs, one at a time, beating well after each addition. Then add the cooled chocolate and the vanilla and mix until blended.

Reduce the speed to low and beat in the flour mixture in three batches, alternating with the milk and beginning and ending with the flour.

Divide the batter evenly among the prepared pans. Tap them on a countertop to rid the batter of any air pockets. Bake until a wooden skewer inserted into the center of each cake comes out clean, 25–30 minutes. Transfer to racks and let cool in the pans for 15 minutes, then invert the cakes onto the racks to cool.

Meanwhile, for the frosting, in a heavy saucepan over high heat, bring the cream to a boil. Remove from the heat and add the chocolate, butter and vanilla, stirring constantly until both the chocolate and butter are melted and the mixture is smooth.

Place the pan in the refrigerator and stir every 15 minutes. The frosting will begin to set after about 50 minutes. Check every 5 minutes near this point for a spreadable consistency. (If the frosting becomes too thick, let it stand at room temperature, stirring occasionally, until it softens and becomes spreadable.)

To frost the cakes, place 1 cake layer, flat side up, on a 12-inch (30-cm) cake plate. Spread the top with one-fourth of the frosting. Place the second cake layer, flat side up, on top of the first and flatten gently with your hand. Spread the top of the second layer with one-third of the remaining frosting. Place the third layer, flat side up, on top and again flatten gently.

Frost the top and sides of the cake quickly, using all of the remaining frosting. Using a flat-edged knife or icing spatula, make quick movements to create swirls on the top and sides of the cake. Let stand for about 1 hour to set the frosting, then serve at room temperature.

Serves 10 to 12

About Vanilla

Vanilla is one of the most common flavorings for cookies, cakes, ice creams, custards and puddings. Real vanilla comes from the bean, or pod, of a climbing orchid, *Vanilla planifolia*, which is native to tropical American forests. The beans are harvested unripe, when they are yellow and have no vanilla flavor. They are then packed tightly and allowed to sweat, which causes the flavor to develop through enzyme activity and the beans to go black. The best-quality beans also acquire a white frosting of strongly aromatic vanillin crystals.

Because they are hand-pollinated and hand-picked, the beans are expensive, but if used whole (for example, when steeped in a hot liquid), they may be rinsed and reused several times. Some recipes call for the bean to be halved lengthwise and its tiny seeds scraped out and added, with the pod, to the liquid in the recipe. Other recipes require vanilla extract (essence), which is made commercially by steeping chopped beans in alcohol and water and allowing the solution to age. Buy only pure vanilla extract; imitation vanilla is made of artificial flavorings and has a crude, inferior taste.

Vanilla beans should be stored in an airtight jar, or in the plastic cylinder in which they were bought, in a cool, dark place for up to 1 year. The tightly capped extract will keep indefinitely in a cool, dark place.

Tiramisu

5 eggs, separated

¼ cup (2 oz/60 g) sugar

2 cups (1 lb/480 g)
mascarpone cheese

¼ cup (2 fl oz/60 ml) dark rum

¾ cup (6 fl oz/180 ml)
very strong black coffee

24 sponge finger cookies
(savoiardi/ladyfingers)

2 oz (60 g) grated milk chocolate
or unsweetened cocoa powder

In a bowl, whisk the egg yolks and sugar until pale and thick. Fold in the mascarpone and rum. With an electric mixer on medium to high speed, beat the egg whites until soft peaks form. Stir one-third of the egg whites into the mascarpone mixture. Gently fold in the remaining egg whites.

Pour the coffee into a bowl. Dip each sponge finger cookie into the coffee for 1–2 seconds. Line the base of a large serving dish, or individual glasses, with half of the sponge finger cookies. Gently spread the mascarpone mixture over the sponge fingers.

Sprinkle with half of the grated chocolate or cocoa. Repeat with the remaining coffee, sponge finger cookies, mascarpone and chocolate or cocoa. Refrigerate overnight and serve chilled.

Serves 6 to 8

Chocolate and Hazelnut Torte

1½ cups (7½ oz/225 g) hazelnuts

1 cup (4 oz/120 g) confectioners' (icing) sugar

3 tablespoons potato starch (potato flour)

⅔ cup (3½ oz/105 g) unbleached all-purpose (plain) flour

1½ tablespoons unsweetened cocoa powder

2½ teaspoons baking powder

Pinch of ground cinnamon

½ cup (4 oz/120 g) unsalted butter, cut into small pieces

2 extra-large eggs, slightly beaten, plus 1 extra-large egg yolk

2 teaspoons vanilla extract (essence)

Preheat an oven to 325°F (165°C/Gas Mark 3).

Spread the hazelnuts in a single layer on a baking sheet and toast in the oven until they just begin to change color and the skins begin to loosen, 8–10 minutes. Spread the warm nuts on a kitchen towel. Cover with another kitchen towel and rub the nuts to remove as much of the skin as possible. Let cool.

Raise the oven temperature to 450°F (230°C/Gas Mark 6). Butter and flour a 9-inch (23-cm) round cake pan.

CHOCOLATE AND HAZELNUT TORTE

In a food processor fitted with a metal blade or in a blender, combine ½ cup (2½ oz/75 g) of the peeled, cooled hazelnuts and the confectioners' sugar. Process just until the hazelnuts are finely ground, almost to a flour. Do not overprocess.

In a bowl, combine the ground nut mixture, the potato starch, all-purpose flour, cocoa, baking powder and cinnamon. Using an electric mixer on medium speed, beat for a few seconds to aerate the flour mixture. Add the butter and continue to beat until the butter is in very small pieces. Beat in the whole eggs

and the egg yolk and the vanilla until blended. Increase the speed to medium-high and beat until the mixture is fluffy and a light cocoa color, 2–3 minutes.

Pour the batter into the pan and level the surface. Place in the center of the oven and immediately reduce the heat to 400°F (200°C/Gas Mark 5). Bake until a wooden skewer inserted in the center comes out clean, 30–35 minutes.

While the cake is baking, place the remaining 1 cup (5 oz/ 150 g) hazelnuts in the food processor fitted with the metal

blade or the blender. Process just until the hazelnuts are coarsely ground.

When the cake is done, transfer it to a rack; let cool for 5 minutes. Run a sharp knife around the edge of the pan to loosen the cake sides and invert the cake onto the rack. Then place, right side up, on a serving plate. Immediately sprinkle the ground hazelnuts evenly over the top and press lightly to adhere. Let cool completely and serve.

Serves 8

About Hazelnuts

Hazelnuts, also known as cobnuts or filberts, are crisp and sweet. They are usually sold shelled as their shells are hard to crack. Their round shape makes them ideal for candying whole, and using as a decoration for desserts. Or, they can be sliced by hand with a small serrated knife (leave their skin on for color contrast and added flavor) and used as an attractive and delicious topping. Ground hazelnuts can replace flour in some recipes and will result in very moist cakes. Hazelnuts may be used whole or chopped, with their skin on, or they may be toasted and skinned (see page 68).

When toasting hazelnuts, stir often, to make sure they don't burn. Their skins are thinner than those of almonds, and don't slip off so easily. After toasting the nuts, put them into a paper bag, or wrap in a clean cloth and rub them against one another. If you want to remove the skins without toasting the nuts, put them in a bowl and pour boiling water over them. Leave for about 5 minutes, drain and remove the skins with a knife.

Always store hazelnuts in their skins — they will keep much longer. Place them in an airtight container and store them in the refrigerator.

Three-Layer Chocolate Terrine

7 oz (210 g) semisweet (plain)
chocolate

6½ oz (195 g) milk chocolate

5 oz (150 g) white chocolate

3 cups (24 fl oz/720 ml)
heavy (double) cream

Chop the chocolate into small pieces and place each sort in a separate heatproof bowl. Heat the cream to boiling point and pour 1¼ cups (10 fl oz/300 ml) over the semisweet chocolate, 1 cup (8 fl oz/240 ml) over the milk chocolate and ¾ cup (6 fl oz/180 ml) over the white chocolate.

Whisk each chocolate until smooth. Cover each bowl with plastic wrap and cool to room temperature. Refrigerate until thick, but not hardened, about 2½ hours.

Line a 6-inch (15-cm) round springform pan with plastic wrap, leaving a 1-inch (2.5-cm) overhang around the top of the pan. Remove the semisweet chocolate mixture from the fridge and beat, using an electric mixer, until thick, soft peaks form. Pour into the prepared pan, cover with plastic wrap and freeze for at least 5 minutes. Remove the plastic wrap and repeat with the other bowls of chocolate.

Cover the pan with plastic wrap and freeze overnight. Remove the terrine from the freezer 15 minutes before serving. Just before serving, remove the sides of the pan, peel off the plastic wrap and slice into wedges.

Serves 10

73

Java Cream Tart

Tart Pastry (page 17)

2 oz (60 g) semisweet (plain) chocolate, chopped

3 tablespoons butter

¼ cup (2 fl oz/60 ml) whipping cream

1 teaspoon light corn syrup

¾ cup (6 oz/180 g) sugar

3 tablespoons cornstarch (cornflour)

2 teaspoons instant coffee granules

1¾ cups (14 fl oz/420 ml) milk

2 beaten egg yolks

2½ oz (75 g) semisweet (plain) chocolate, chopped

½ teaspoon vanilla extract (essence)

½ cup (4 fl oz/120 ml) whipping cream, whipped, to serve

Chocolate curls, to garnish

Preheat an oven to 375°F (190°C/Gas Mark 4).

Prepare pastry as directed. Roll into a 13-inch (32-cm) circle. Ease pastry into an 11-inch (28-cm) tart pan with removable bottom. Press pastry into fluted sides of tart pan and trim pastry even with the edge. Prick pastry and line with a double thickness of aluminum foil. Bake for 10 minutes. Remove foil and bake for 5–10 minutes more, or until light brown. Cool in tart pan on a rack.

Meanwhile, in a double boiler or in a heatproof bowl set over (not touching) simmering water in a pan, melt the 2 oz (60 g) chocolate and 1 tablespoon of the butter over low heat. In a heavy saucepan, stir together ¼ cup (2 fl oz/60 ml) whipping cream and the corn syrup. Bring to a gentle boil. Reduce heat and cook for 2 minutes more. Remove from heat; stir in the chocolate mixture. Cool to room temperature. Spread cooled mixture over the bottom and up the sides of the pastry shell.

In a medium saucepan, combine the sugar, cornstarch and coffee granules. Stir in milk. Cook and stir over medium heat until the mixture is thick and bubbly. Cook and stir for 2 minutes more. Remove from the heat. Gradually stir about half of the hot mixture into the beaten egg yolks. Return all to saucepan. Cook and stir until bubbly. Reduce heat. Cook and stir for 2 minutes more. Remove from heat. Stir in 2½ oz (75 g) chopped chocolate, the remaining 2 tablespoons of the butter, and the vanilla, until the chocolate is melted. Pour into pastry shell. Cover surface with plastic wrap. Chill for 4–24 hours, or until firm. To serve, carefully remove plastic wrap and sides of pan. Pipe whipped cream over top of pie. Garnish with chocolate curls.

Serves 8

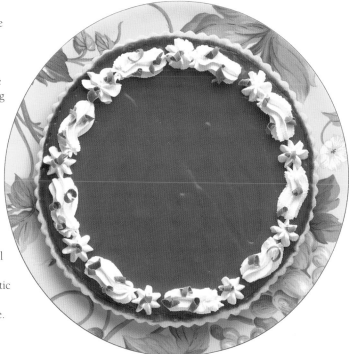

Pavlova with Chocolate Hazelnut Cream

MERINGUE

8 egg whites, at room temperature

1½ cups (12 oz/360 g) sugar

CHOCOLATE HAZELNUT CREAM

1¼ cups (10 fl oz/300 ml) heavy (double) cream, whipped

1 cup (4 oz/120 g) ground hazelnuts

4 oz (120 g) semisweet (plain) chocolate, melted and cooled

¼ cup (1 oz/30 g) chopped hazelnuts

Preheat an oven to 250°F (120°C/Gas Mark 1). Line a baking sheet with parchment (baking) paper.

For the meringue, in a large bowl beat the egg whites until soft peaks form. Add ½ cup (4 oz/120 g) of the sugar and beat. Continue beating and adding the remaining sugar until stiff peaks form and the sugar completely dissolves.

Using a spatula, shape the meringue into two 8-inch (20-cm) rounds on the baking sheet. Make a dip in the center of one (for the bottom layer) and a peak in the center of the other (for the top layer).

Bake for 10 minutes. Reduce the heat to 225°F (110°C/Gas Mark ½) and bake for another 45–50 minutes, until meringues sound hollow when gently tapped. Remove from the oven and allow to cool on a rack.

For the chocolate hazelnut cream, fold together the cream, ground hazelnuts and half of the melted chocolate. Spread the bottom round of the meringue with the cream mixture and top with the remaining meringue round. Drizzle or pipe with the remaining chocolate and sprinkle with the chopped hazelnuts.

Serves 8

Chocolate and Banana Cream Pie

Fully baked single-crust pastry shell (page 12)

FILLING

¾ cup (6 oz/180 g) sugar

½ cup (2½ oz/75 g) all-purpose (plain) flour

3 cups (24 fl oz/720 ml) milk

3 oz (90 g) semisweet (plain) chocolate, chopped

4 beaten egg yolks

1 tablespoon butter

1½ teaspoons vanilla extract (essence)

¼ to ½ teaspoon almond extract (essence) (optional)

3 medium bananas, sliced

MERINGUE

4 egg whites

½ teaspoon vanilla extract (essence)

¼ teaspoon cream of tartar

½ cup (4 oz/120 g) sugar

Prepare and bake pastry shell as directed; set aside.

Preheat an oven to 350°F (180°C/Gas Mark 4).

For the filling, in a heavy, medium pan stir together the sugar and flour. Gradually stir in the milk. Add the chocolate. Cook and stir over medium heat until the mixture is thick and bubbly. Reduce heat. Cook and stir for 2 minutes more. Remove from the heat.

Gradually stir about 1 cup of the hot mixture into the beaten egg yolks. Return all to pan. Bring to a gentle boil. Cook and stir for 2 minutes more. Remove from heat. Stir in butter, vanilla and, if desired, almond extract. Arrange banana slices over the bottom of the baked pastry shell; pour hot filling over the banana.

For the meringue, in a bowl combine egg whites, vanilla and cream of tartar. Beat with an electric mixer on medium speed for about 1 minute, or until soft peaks form. Gradually add the sugar, 1 tablespoon at a time, beating on high speed about 4 minutes more or until stiff peaks form and sugar completely dissolves. Immediately spread the meringue over the hot pie filling, carefully spreading the meringue to the edge of pastry to seal and prevent any shrinkage.

Bake for 15 minutes. Cool on a rack for 1 hour. Chill for 3–6 hours before serving. Store in refrigerator.

Serves 8

Espresso French Silk Pie

Fully baked single-crust pastry shell (page 12)

3 oz (90 g) unsweetened (bitter) chocolate, chopped

2–3 teaspoons instant coffee granules

¾ cup (6 oz/180 g) butter, softened

1 cup (8 oz/240 g) sugar

1 teaspoon vanilla extract (essence)

3 eggs

½ cup (4 fl oz/120 ml) whipped cream (optional), to serve

Strawberry fans (optional), to serve

Prepare and bake the pastry shell as directed; set aside.

Combine the chocolate and coffee granules in a heavy, small saucepan. Heat over very low heat, stirring constantly until the chocolate begins to melt. Remove pan from heat and stir until smooth. Set aside to cool.

In a large bowl, beat the butter and sugar with an electric mixer on medium speed, 4–5 minutes. Stir in the melted chocolate mixture and the vanilla. Add the eggs, one at a time, beating on high speed after each, and scraping the sides of the bowl.

Spoon the filling into the baked pastry shell. Cover and chill in the refrigerator for 5–24 hours, or until set. Garnish with the whipped cream and strawberry fans, if desired.

Serves 10

Chocolate Bread Pudding

6 cups (12 oz/360 g) cubed bread, preferably French or egg bread (¾-inch/2-cm cubes)

4 oz (120 g) unsweetened (bitter) chocolate, chopped

3 cups (24 fl oz/720 ml) milk

3 eggs

1¼ cups (10 oz/300 g) granulated sugar

2 teaspoons vanilla extract (essence)

2 tablespoons confectioners' (icing) sugar

Whipped cream (optional), to serve

Preheat an oven to 350°F (180°C/Gas Mark 4). Butter a 1½-qt (1.4-l) soufflé dish or baking dish.

Spread the bread cubes on a baking sheet. Bake until dry but not browned, 5–7 minutes. Remove from the oven and set aside.

In the top pan of a double boiler or in a heatproof bowl set over (not touching) simmering water in a pan, combine the chocolate and milk and stir until the chocolate melts and the mixture is smooth, 5–7 minutes. Remove

from the heat and let cool for 10 minutes.

In a bowl, using an electric mixer on high speed, beat the eggs until blended. Add the granulated sugar and beat until slightly thickened, 1–2 minutes. Reduce the speed to low and gradually beat in the vanilla and the chocolate-milk mixture until combined.

Place the bread cubes in the soufflé or baking dish. Pour the chocolate custard over the bread and, using a spoon, turn the mixture so that all the bread cubes are evenly soaked with the custard mixture.

Bake for 20 minutes. Then, using the back of a large spoon, push down on the bread so the custard rises to the top. Continue baking until the custard is just set, 15–20 minutes longer.

Transfer to a rack and, using a sieve or sifter, lightly dust the top with the confectioners' sugar. Serve warm or at room temperature with whipped cream, if desired.

Serves 6

Mississippi Mud Cake

1 cup (8 oz/240 g) unsalted butter

1 tablespoon whiskey

¾ cup (6 oz/180 g) sugar

8 oz (240 g) semisweet (plain) chocolate, chopped

1½ cups (12 fl oz/360 ml) hot water

1½ cups (6 oz/180 g) self-rising flour

¼ cup (1 oz/30 g) unsweetened cocoa powder

2 eggs

1 teaspoon vanilla extract (essence)

Heavy (double) cream (optional), to serve

Preheat an oven to 350°F (180°C/Gas Mark 4). Butter a 9-inch (23-cm) round cake pan and line the base with parchment (baking) paper.

Melt the butter in a saucepan. Add whiskey, sugar, chocolate and water. Stir over low heat until the chocolate is just melted and the mixture is smooth.

Sift the flour and cocoa powder together and gradually beat into the chocolate mixture. Add the eggs and vanilla and beat until combined. Pour the mixture into the cake pan and bake for 40–45 minutes, until a wooden skewer inserted in the center comes out clean.

Leave the cake in the pan for 15 minutes before turning out to cool. Serve warm or cold with cream, if desired.

Serves 8 to 10

White Chocolate Berry Cake

CAKE

6 egg yolks

1 cup (8 fl oz/240 ml) milk

1 teaspoon vanilla extract (essence)

3⅓ cups (13 oz/390 g) self-rising flour

1 cup (8 oz/240 g) sugar

½ cup (4 oz/120 g) butter, softened

5½ oz (165 g) white chocolate, melted

FILLING AND TOPPING

9½ oz (285 g) white chocolate, melted

2 cups (1 lb/480 g) mixed summer berries

Preheat an oven to 350°F (180°C/Gas Mark 4). Butter two 9-inch (23-cm) springform cake pans and line bases with parchment (baking) paper.

For the cake, combine the egg yolks, ¼ cup (2 fl oz/60 ml) of the milk, and the vanilla, in a bowl. In a large bowl, combine the flour and sugar. Add the butter and the remaining ¾ cup (6 fl oz/180 ml) milk. Beat on low speed until well combined, 3–4 minutes. Gradually add the egg mixture in 3 batches, beating well after each addition. Add the melted chocolate and beat to combine, about 2 minutes. Pour the mixture into the pans.

Bake for 35–40 minutes, or until a wooden skewer inserted in the center of each cake comes out clean. Let cool in the pan for 10 minutes before turning onto a rack to cool completely.

For the filling and topping, spread one-third of the warm melted chocolate over 1 cake layer using a large spatula. Place the berries, reserving a few for decoration, on top of the cake layer spread with the chocolate. Place the second cake layer on top and cover the assembled cake with the remaining melted white chocolate. Decorate with the reserved berries and serve.

Serves 10 to 12

Chocolate and Nut Torte

1½ cups (7½ oz/225 g) almonds and hazelnuts

8 oz (240 g) semisweet (plain) chocolate, chopped

6 egg whites

Pinch of salt

⅓ cup (2½ oz/75 g) superfine (caster) sugar

½ cup (3 oz/90 g) chopped candied (glacéed) figs

½ cup (3 oz/90 g) chopped dried dates

⅓ cup (2 oz/60 g) chopped candied (glacéed) apricots

Preheat an oven to 350°F (180°C/Gas Mark 4). Butter a 9-inch (23-cm) springform cake pan and line with aluminum foil.

Place the almonds, hazelnuts and chocolate into a food processor and process until fine.

Beat together the egg whites with a pinch of salt until soft peaks form. Gradually add the sugar and continue beating until stiff peaks form and the sugar is completely dissolved.

Stir one-third of the chocolate and nut mixture and one-third of the fruit into the egg-white mixture. Gently fold through the remaining chocolate and fruit. Pour into the pan and bake for 45 minutes.

After 45 minutes, turn off the oven and allow the torte to cool in the oven with the door ajar. When cooled, turn out and wrap in plastic wrap or aluminum foil. Refrigerate overnight.

Serves 8 to 10

Chocolate Truffle Tart

Tart Pastry (page 17)

FILLING

¾ cup (6 oz/180 g) unsalted butter

½ cup (4 oz/120 g) sugar

6 eggs

1¼ lb (600 g) semisweet (plain) chocolate, melted and cooled

¼ cup (2 fl oz/60 ml) light (single) cream

1 teaspoon vanilla extract (essence)

TRUFFLES

5½ oz (165 g) semisweet (plain) chocolate, finely chopped

⅔ cup (5 fl oz/150 ml) heavy (double) cream

1 tablespoon unsalted butter

½ cup (1½ oz/45 g) unsweetened cocoa powder

Prepare the pastry as directed. Roll out the pastry and fit into a 10-inch (25-cm) tart pan. Refrigerate for 30 minutes.

Preheat an oven to 400°F (200°C/Gas Mark 5).

Line the pastry with a sheet of aluminum foil and weigh down with baking weights, dried beans or rice. Bake the pastry shell for 10 minutes. Reduce the temperature to 350°F (180°C/Gas Mark 4) and then bake for another 10 minutes. Remove the foil and weights and bake for 10 minutes more, until the pastry is golden brown. Allow the pastry to cool completely.

CHOCOLATE TRUFFLE TART

For the filling, cream the butter and sugar until fluffy. Beat in the eggs, 1 at a time, beating well after each addition. Continue beating for another 2 minutes, until the mixture has lightened in color and has increased in volume. Whisk in the cooled chocolate. Stir in the cream and vanilla. Pour the filling into the cooled pastry shell and refrigerate for at least 6 hours.

For the truffles, place the chocolate pieces in a bowl. Combine the cream and butter in a saucepan and bring just to boiling point. Pour this mixture over the chocolate and stir well until the chocolate is melted and smooth. Set aside to cool. Cover and refrigerate until the mixture is hard enough to roll into balls, about 40 minutes.

Dust your hands with a little cocoa and roll teaspoonfuls of the mixture into small balls. Roll the truffles in some more cocoa and leave in a cool place until needed.

Just before serving, remove the tart from the refrigerator and decorate with the truffles.

Serves 10 to 12

About Chocolate

Chocolate was enjoyed as a drink by the Aztecs long before the Spaniards arrived in Mexico. *Chocolatl* was first brought to Spain by Cortes in 1528, and the first chocolate house opened in London in 1657, but the high customs duty imposed on cocoa meant that it was only the very rich who could afford it until the mid-nineteenth century.

Theobroma cacao, the tree that provides chocolate, is native to tropical America, but is now cultivated worldwide in equatorial regions. Its beans are fermented, roasted, shelled and crushed into small "nibs." The nibs—which contain more than 50 percent cocoa butter, the fat of chocolate—are ground and compressed into a mass called chocolate liquor. With a little further refining, this becomes unsweetened (bitter) chocolate. Depending on how much sugar is added, the chocolate liquor becomes bittersweet, semisweet or sweet chocolate. These are all types of dark (plain) chocolate; the addition of milk solids produces milk chocolate. When about three-fourths of the cocoa butter is removed and the remaining chocolate liquor is ground into powder, it becomes cocoa powder.

The better the chocolate you use in your recipes, the better the result. One of the finest types is couverture. Avoid "compound" chocolate; this is cheaper than other chocolate because some of the cocoa butter has been replaced with oil, which changes the taste and texture. The best chocolate to use in cooking is semisweet (plain) chocolate, unless the recipe specifically calls for another type.

Mexican Chocolate Soufflés

2 tablespoons butter

⅓ cup (2 oz/60 g) confectioners' (icing) sugar

3½ oz (105 g) bittersweet (plain) chocolate

2 tablespoons granulated sugar

3 tablespoons milk

¼ teaspoon ground cinnamon

1 teaspoon vanilla extract (essence)

2 egg yolks

3 egg whites

⅓ cup (2 oz/60 g) almonds, toasted and finely ground

Custard (optional), to serve

Preheat the oven to 400°F (200°C/Gas Mark 5).

Butter 4 individual soufflé molds (3 inches/7.5 cm) in diameter x 1¾ inches (4.5 cm) deep, and dust with half of the confectioners' sugar.

Melt the chocolate in a double boiler or in a heatproof bowl set over (not touching) simmering water in a pan, with 1 tablespoon of the sugar, the milk, cinnamon and vanilla. Remove from the heat and let cool slightly. Add the egg yolks and blend well.

In a separate bowl, beat the egg whites with the remaining granulated sugar until soft peaks form. Fold into the chocolate mixture, alternating with the ground almonds.

Fill the molds to within ½ inch (1 cm) of the rim, allowing room for the soufflé to rise. Bake for 10 minutes or until firm but still soft in the center.

To serve, unmold the soufflés by running a sharp knife around the sides of each mold, then turn upside down onto a dessert plate. Sprinkle the top of each soufflé with the remaining confectioners' sugar. Serve with custard, if desired.

Makes 4

German Chocolate Strudel Braid

STRUDEL BRAID

1 slightly beaten egg white

½ cup (2 oz/60 g) ground pecans

½ cup (1½ oz/45 g) flaked coconut

2 oz (60 g) milk chocolate, chopped

¼ cup (4 oz/120 g) sugar

2 tablespoons milk

¼ teaspoon vanilla extract (essence)

6 sheets frozen filo dough (about 18- × 12-inch/50- × 30-cm rectangles), thawed

¼ cup (2 oz/60 g) butter, melted

TOPPING

¼ cup (¾ oz/20 g) coconut

¼ cup (1 oz/30 g) chopped pecans

⅓ cup (3 oz/90 g) sugar

¼ cup (2 fl oz/60 ml) water

2 tablespoons honey

To toast the coconut and pecans for the topping, spread on separate baking sheets and bake in a 350°F (180°C/Gas Mark 4) oven for 5–10 minutes or until light golden brown. Remove.

Increase the oven temperature to 375°F (190°C/Gas Mark 4).

For the strudel braid, in a bowl combine the egg white, ground pecans, coconut, chocolate, sugar, milk and vanilla; set filling aside. Unfold filo dough; remove 1 sheet. (Cover remaining dough with plastic wrap to prevent drying.) Place the sheet on a large greased baking sheet. Brush with some of the melted butter. Layer another sheet on the first, brushing top with butter. Repeat with remaining sheets and butter. Evenly trim the edges.

On both long sides, use scissors to make 4½-inch (12-cm) cuts from edge toward center, spacing the cuts 1 inch (2.5 cm) apart. Spoon the filling lengthwise down the uncut center of the filo stack. Starting at one end, fold and slightly twist the filo strips at an angle over the filling. Tuck ends under. Brush top with remaining butter. Bake for 20–25 minutes, or until golden.

For the topping, combine sugar, water and honey. Bring to boiling. Reduce heat and simmer, uncovered, for 3 minutes. Transfer braid to a wire rack over a tray. Gradually spoon the sugar mixture over the braid, allowing it to soak in. Sprinkle with toasted coconut and pecans. Cool and serve.

Serves 10 to 12

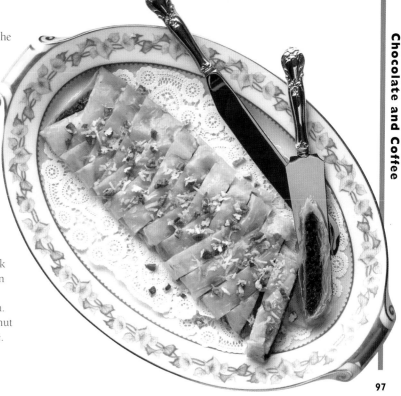

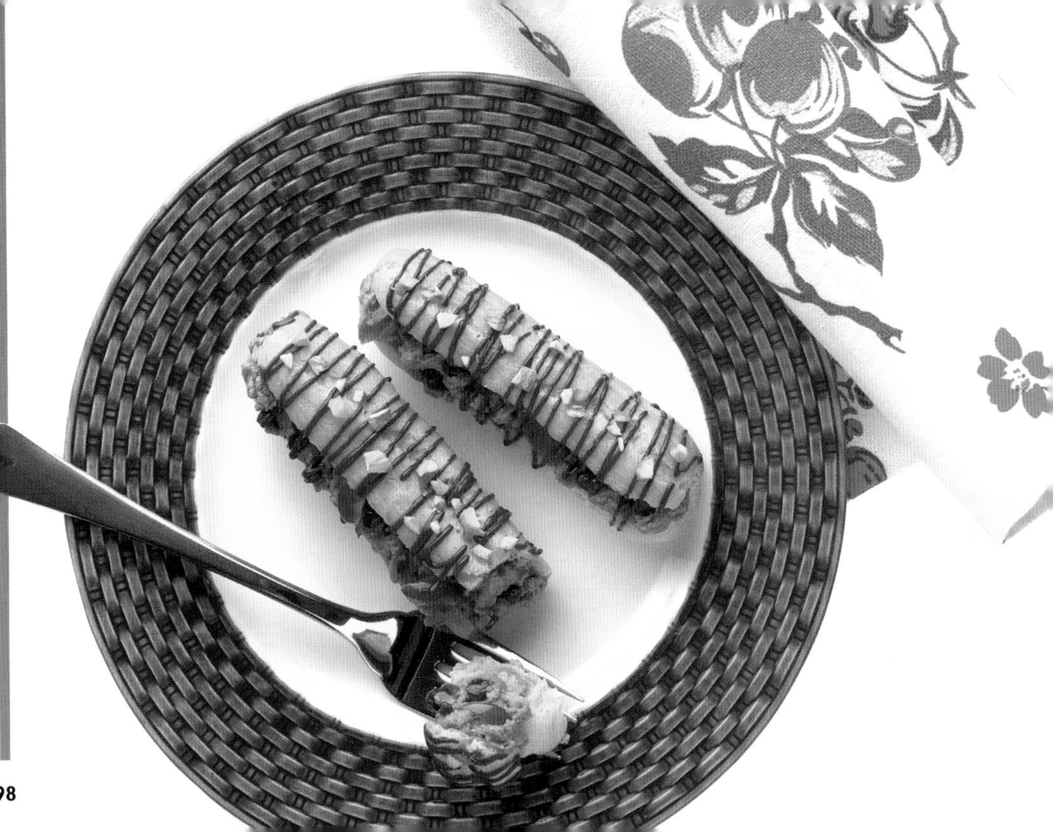

Chocolate Cannoli Éclairs

Cream Puff Pastry (page 24)

FILLING

2 cups (1 lb/480 g) ricotta cheese

¼ cup (2 oz/60 g) sugar

4 teaspoons unsweetened cocoa powder

1 teaspoon vanilla extract (essence)

2 oz (60 g) semisweet (plain) chocolate, chopped

3 tablespoons chopped candied (glacéed) cherries

TOPPING

2 oz (60 g) semisweet (plain) chocolate, chopped

1 tablespoon butter

1 teaspoon light corn syrup

¼ cup (1 oz/30 g) chopped pistachio nuts

Preheat an oven to 400°F (200°C/Gas Mark 5).

Prepare cream puff pastry as directed, except spoon dough into a decorating bag fitted with a large plain round tip (about a ½-inch/1-cm opening). Slowly pipe strips of dough 3 inches (7.5 cm) apart onto a lightly greased baking sheet, making 12 éclairs, each about 4 inches (10 cm) long, 1¼ inches (3 cm) wide and ¾ inch (2 cm) high.

Bake for 30–35 minutes, or until golden brown. Remove from tray and cool on a rack.

For the filling, in a bowl, stir together ricotta cheese, sugar, cocoa and vanilla until smooth. Fold in chocolate and cherries. Cover and chill.

Up to 1 hour before serving, horizontally cut the éclairs in half. Remove any soft dough from the insides. Fill with ricotta filling. Replace tops.

For the topping, melt chocolate, butter and corn syrup over low heat; drizzle over éclairs. Sprinkle with nuts. Chill.

Makes 12

Chocolate Crepes
with Mascarpone and Toffee

CREPES

2 eggs

¼ cup (2 oz/60 g) sugar

1 cup (8 fl oz/240 ml) milk

½ cup (2½ oz/75 g) all-purpose (plain) flour, sifted

1 tablespoon unsweetened cocoa powder

Pinch of salt

3 tablespoons unsalted butter, melted

TOFFEE

1 cup (8 oz/240 g) sugar

1 cup (8 fl oz/240 ml) water

1 cup (8 oz/240 g) mascarpone cheese

CHOCOLATE SAUCE

5 oz (150 g) semisweet (plain) chocolate

2 tablespoons unsalted butter

½ cup (4 fl oz/120 ml) heavy (double) cream

1 tablespoon brandy (optional)

For the crepes, place the eggs in a large bowl and beat well. Beat in the sugar, milk, flour, cocoa, salt and 2 tablespoons of the melted butter. Cover and let stand for 30 minutes.

For the toffee, lightly oil a baking sheet. Combine the sugar and water in a saucepan. Stir over low heat until the sugar dissolves. Bring to a boil and boil until golden, 5–7 minutes. Pour the toffee onto the baking sheet and tilt

Chocolate and Coffee

so that the toffee forms a thin layer. Let cool and harden for 10 minutes.

Remove the toffee pieces from the baking sheet, place in a small bowl and crush the toffee with a spoon. Stir three-fourths of the crushed toffee into the mascarpone. Set aside the remainder for decoration.

For the chocolate sauce, melt the chocolate and butter over simmering water in a double boiler or in a heatproof bowl set over (not touching) simmering water in a pan. Stir in the cream until completely blended. Flavor with the brandy, if desired.

Heat a crepe pan or 8-inch (20-cm) nonstick frying pan over moderate heat. Brush the bottom of the pan with some of the remaining 1 tablespoon of melted butter. Pour in 2 tablespoons of the crepe batter and tilt the pan to spread the batter evenly and thinly. Cook for 2–3 minutes until the crepe is just set on top and brown underneath. Turn to the other side and cook for 1 minute. Remove to a plate and repeat until all of the mixture is used, making at least 6 crepes.

Stack the cooked crepes on a plate with a piece of parchment

(baking) or waxed (greaseproof) paper between each crepe. Keep the whole plate covered with a clean dish towel. When all of the crepes are cooked, place 1 tablespoon of the mascarpone and toffee mixture in the center of each crepe. Fold the sides over so that it looks like a pillow. Serve each crepe drizzled with chocolate sauce and sprinkled with extra toffee.

Serves 6

102

White Mousse Tart with Raspberry Sauce

CHOCOLATE PASTRY

1¼ cups (6½ oz/195 g) all-purpose (plain) flour

2 tablespoons sugar

2 tablespoons unsweetened cocoa powder

¼ teaspoon salt

½ cup (4 oz/120 g) vegetable shortening or butter

4–5 tablespoons water

FILLING

½ cup (4 oz/120 g) sugar

1 tablespoon (1 envelope) gelatin

1⅓ cups (11 fl oz/330 ml) milk

3 slightly beaten egg yolks

1¼ cups (6 oz/180 g) white chocolate, chopped

½ cup (4 fl oz/120 ml) whipping cream

RASPBERRY SAUCE

2½ cups (10 oz/300 g) frozen raspberries, thawed

Water

1 tablespoon cornstarch (cornflour)

⅓ cup (3½ oz/105 g) redcurrant jelly

WHITE MOUSSE TART WITH RASPBERRY SAUCE

Chocolate and Coffee

Preheat an oven to 450°F (220°C/Gas Mark 6).

For the chocolate pastry, in a medium bowl stir together flour, sugar, cocoa and salt. Cut in vegetable shortening or butter until pieces are the size of small peas. Sprinkle water, 1 tablespoon at a time, over dough, tossing with a fork until all is moistened. Form dough into a ball. On a lightly floured surface, roll dough into a 13-inch (32-cm) circle. Ease pastry into an 11-inch (28-cm) tart pan with a removable bottom. Press pastry into fluted sides of tart pan; trim pastry even with the edge of the tart pan. Line unpricked pastry

shell with a double thickness of aluminum foil. Bake for 12–15 minutes, or until pastry is set and dry. Cool on a rack.

For the filling, in a medium saucepan combine sugar and gelatin. Stir in milk and egg yolks. Cook and stir over medium heat until gelatin dissolves and mixture thickens slightly and just begins to bubble. Stir in chocolate just until melted. Set the saucepan in a large bowl of ice water for about 15 minutes, or until partially set, stirring frequently. Or, transfer gelatin mixture to a bowl; chill about 1 hour, or until partially set, stirring occasionally (start watching

mixture closely after about 40 minutes). Beat whipping cream until soft peaks form; fold whipped cream into gelatin mixture. Transfer filling to cooled pastry shell. Chill for 4–24 hours, or until firm.

For the raspberry sauce, drain raspberries, reserving syrup. Add water to syrup to equal ¾ cup (6 fl oz/180 ml). In a small saucepan combine syrup mixture and cornstarch. Stir in redcurrant jelly. Cook and stir over medium heat until thickened. Cook and stir for 2 minutes more. Stir in the raspberries. Chill well, then serve with the tart.

Serves 8

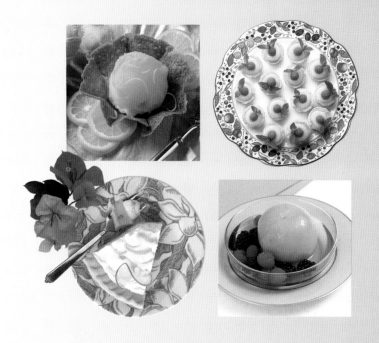

FRUIT

Plum Tart with Toasted Almonds

Sweet Pastry Dough (page 20)

2 cups (16 fl oz/480 ml) pastry cream (page 27)

½ cup (4 oz/120 g) almond paste

¾ cup (6 oz/180 g) sugar

½ cup (4 oz/120 g) unsalted butter, at room temperature

2 whole eggs, plus 1 egg yolk

½ cup (2 oz/60 g) cake (soft-wheat) flour

8–10 red plums, pitted and sliced

¼ cup (2½ oz/75 g) apricot jam

3 tablespoons blanched sliced (flaked) almonds, toasted

Prepare the pastry dough and pastry cream as directed and refrigerate the dough for 1 hour.

Preheat an oven to 375°F (190°C/Gas Mark 4). Butter and flour a 10-inch (25-cm) tart pan with a removable bottom.

On a lightly floured work surface, roll out the dough into a round ⅛ inch (3 mm) thick. Carefully transfer the dough to the prepared tart pan and press gently into the bottom and sides. Trim the dough even with the pan rim. Refrigerate until ready to assemble the tart.

In a bowl, combine the almond paste and sugar. Using an electric mixer, beat on medium speed until combined, about 2 minutes. Add the butter and beat for 6 minutes on medium speed until light and smooth.

Add the whole eggs one at a time, beating well after each addition. Add the egg yolk and mix until smooth, about 30 seconds longer. Add the cake flour and beat on low speed just until combined. Add the pastry cream and beat on low speed to combine, about 1 minute.

Spoon the batter into the tart shell. Arrange the plums, cut sides down, on top of the batter, pressing the plums in slightly. Place the tart on a baking sheet. Bake until the batter has set and the pastry is golden brown, 35–45 minutes. Transfer to a rack and let cool, 5–10 minutes. Remove the pan sides and slide the tart from the pan bottom.

In a small saucepan over a medium heat, melt the apricot jam. Using a pastry brush, lightly brush the warm jam over the surface. Garnish with the toasted almonds. Serve warm.

Serves 8 to 10

Strawberry Tortoni

3 cups (24 fl oz/720 ml) heavy (double) cream

3 cups (12 oz/360 g) strawberries, roughly chopped

¾ cup (3 oz/90 g) slivered almonds, toasted

9 amaretti cookies, crushed

⅓ cup (2½ fl oz/75 ml) brandy

3 egg whites

¾ cup (6 oz/180 g) superfine (caster) sugar

½ teaspoon baking powder

Extra amaretti cookies (optional), to serve

Whip the cream and set aside. Mix the strawberries, almonds, crushed amaretti cookies and brandy in a bowl. Set aside for 10 minutes.

With an electric mixer set on medium to high speed, beat the egg whites until soft peaks form. Slowly add the sugar and baking powder. Continue to beat the eggs until stiff peaks form.

Fold the beaten egg whites and the strawberry mixture into the cream, combining thoroughly.

Pour the strawberry mixture into individual serving dishes or the desired mold and freeze, covered, for 4–5 hours. Serve frozen with additional amaretti cookies, if desired.

Makes 6

Pear and Cinnamon Teacake

CAKE

1 egg, separated

½ cup (4 oz/120 g) sugar

½ cup (4 fl oz/120 ml) milk

½ teaspoon vanilla extract (essence)

2 tablespoons butter, melted

1 cup (4 oz/120 g) self-rising flour, sifted

1 pear, peeled, cored and thinly sliced

TOPPING

1 tablespoon butter, melted

½ teaspoon ground cinnamon

1 tablespoon sugar

Heavy (double) cream or butter (optional), to serve

Preheat an oven to 375°F (190°C/Gas Mark 4). Butter an 8-inch (20-cm) round cake pan.

For the cake, whisk the egg white until stiff peaks form. Gradually beat in the sugar, then the egg yolk. Stir in the milk, vanilla and melted butter. Gently fold in the flour, then pour the mixture into the prepared pan.

Arrange the pear slices in a fan shape on top of the mixture. Bake for 20–25 minutes, or until a skewer inserted in the middle of the cake comes out clean.

Allow the cake to cool in the cake pan for 10 minutes before turning out onto a serving plate.

For the topping, brush the top of the hot cake generously with the melted butter. Combine the cinnamon and sugar and then sprinkle over the top. Serve the cake warm or cold with cream, or spread with butter, if desired.

Serves 8

Baked Bananas with Dark Rum Sauce

1 tablespoon butter

2 tablespoons brown sugar

4 ripe bananas, cut in half lengthwise

DARK RUM SAUCE

1 tablespoon grated lemon or lime zest (rind)

2 tablespoons lemon or lime juice

2 tablespoons sugar

3 tablespoons orange marmalade

¼ cup (2 fl oz/60 ml) water

3 tablespoons dark rum, heated

Preheat an oven to 350°F (180°C/Gas Mark 4). Butter an 8- x 8-inch (20- x 20-cm) heatproof baking dish with the butter and sprinkle the base with the brown sugar. Place the bananas in the baking dish.

For the sauce, combine all but the rum in a saucepan and bring to a boil over a medium heat. Remove from the heat and pour the sauce over the bananas.

Bake for 10–15 minutes, then remove the baking dish from the oven, pour the rum over the bananas, ignite and serve immediately.

Serves 4

Sponge Cake with Lemon Curd

CAKE

4 eggs

½ cup (4 oz/120 g) granulated sugar

1 cup (4 oz/120 g) all-purpose (plain) flour

Pinch of salt

¼ cup (2 oz/60 g) unsalted butter, melted and cooled

Grated zest (rind) of 1 lemon

LEMON CURD

½ cup (4 oz/120 g) unsalted butter

⅔ cup (5 fl oz/150 ml) lemon juice

1 cup (8 oz/240 g) granulated sugar

3 whole eggs

3 egg yolks

1 cup (8 fl oz/240 ml) heavy (double) cream, whipped

Confectioners' (icing) sugar, for dusting

Preheat an oven to 350°F (180°C/Gas Mark 4). Butter two 8-inch (20-cm) round cake pans.

For the cake, whisk the eggs and granulated sugar until the mixture is pale yellow and falls in thick ribbons when the whisk is lifted, 3–4 minutes.

Fold in the flour and salt in 2 batches, adding the butter and lemon zest with the final batch.

Pour the mixture into the cake pans. Bake for 20–30 minutes, or until the cakes spring back when touched in the center. Allow each cake to cool in the pan for 5 minutes before turning out onto a wire rack to cool.

For the lemon curd, in a double boiler or in a heatproof bowl set over (not touching) simmering water in a pan, combine butter, lemon juice and granulated sugar. Stir until the sugar dissolves and the butter melts.

Whisk together the whole eggs and egg yolks and gradually pour into the lemon mixture, whisking constantly. Stir over medium heat for 7–10 minutes, or until the curd is thick. Allow the curd to set completely in the refrigerator, about 2 hours.

Spread the top of one cake layer with ½ cup (4 fl oz/120 ml) of the lemon curd and the cream, then place the second layer on top. The remaining quantity of lemon curd may be stored in the refrigerator for up to 1 week. Dust the top of the assembled cake with the confectioners' sugar and serve.

Serves 8

Peaches Poached in Wine

6 ripe but firm peaches

1 bottle (24 fl oz/720 ml) fruity white or red still or sparkling wine or Champagne

⅓–⅔ cup (3–5 oz/90–150 g) sugar

1 vanilla bean, split lengthwise

Mascarpone cheese (optional), to serve

Bring a saucepan three-fourths full of water to a boil. One at a time, dip the peaches into the boiling water for 5 seconds. Lift out with a slotted spoon and, using a sharp paring knife, peel the peaches. Halve each peach and remove the pits.

In a saucepan large enough to hold all the peaches in a single layer, combine the wine, ⅓ cup (3 oz/90 g) of the sugar and the split vanilla bean. Place over low heat and stir until the sugar dissolves. Taste and add more sugar as needed to achieve a pleasant sweetness (see note). Bring to a simmer, add the peaches, and simmer until they are barely tender, 2–5 minutes, depending upon their ripeness.

Transfer the peaches and their poaching liquid to a deep glass bowl (the peaches should be completely covered by the liquid) and let cool to room temperature. Cover tightly with plastic wrap and refrigerate for at least 2 days or for up to 3 days.

To serve, using a slotted spoon, transfer the peach halves to large wineglasses, placing 2 halves in each glass. Half-fill the glasses with the poaching liquid and serve with the mascarpone cheese, if desired.

NOTE The amount of sugar added to a poaching liquid will depend upon the wine's relative dryness; the liquid should be just sweet enough to heighten the fruit's natural sweetness.

Serves 6

Strawberry Pound Cake

CAKE

2 cups (8 oz/240 g) strawberries, hulled and quartered

1½ cups (7½ oz/225 g) all-purpose (plain) flour, sifted

1 cup (8 oz/240 g) butter

1 cup (8 oz/240 g) granulated sugar

4 eggs

Grated zest (rind) of 1 orange

1 teaspoon baking powder

ICING

1 cup (4 oz/120 g) hulled strawberries

1½ tablespoons confectioners' (icing) sugar

1¼ cups (10 fl oz/300 ml) heavy (double) cream, whipped

Extra strawberries, for garnish

Preheat an oven to 350°F (180°C/Gas Mark 4). Butter a 9-inch (23-cm) round cake pan and line the base with parchment (baking) paper.

For the cake, toss the 2 cups (8 oz/240 g) strawberries in a little of the flour, to coat. Cream the butter and granulated sugar. Add the eggs, one at a time, beating well after each. Fold in the orange zest, flour, baking powder and strawberries in 3 batches. Stir well to combine.

Pour the mixture into the cake pan and bake for 50 minutes, or until a skewer inserted into the middle of the cake comes out clean.

Cool in the pan for 10 minutes before turning out onto a wire rack to cool completely.

For the icing, place the 1 cup (4 oz/120 g) strawberries and confectioners' sugar in the bowl of a food processor and process to a purée. Fold in the whipped cream. Ice the cake and decorate with the extra strawberries.

Serves 10 to 12

Peaches and Berries in Toffee Syrup

8 ripe but firm peaches

3 cups (24 fl oz/720 ml) water

2 cups (16 oz/480 g) sugar

2 cups (8 oz/240 g) raspberries

2 cups (8 oz/240 g) blackberries

Bring a saucepan three-fourths full of water to a boil. One at a time, dip the peaches into the boiling water for 5 seconds. Lift out with a slotted spoon and, using a sharp paring knife, peel the peaches.

Place the sugar and 2 cups (16 fl oz/480 ml) of the water in a saucepan. Stir over low heat, without boiling, until the sugar dissolves. Bring to a boil, without stirring, and boil rapidly until the syrup turns a pale golden brown, forming toffee. Remove from the heat. Add the remaining 1 cup (8 fl oz/240 ml) water (take care, as the mixture will spatter), then stir over a medium heat until the toffee melts; remove from the heat.

Place the peaches in a bowl and pour the syrup over. Allow to cool. When ready to serve, arrange peaches and berries in a bowl and spoon syrup over.

Serves 8

Mixed Fruit Clafouti

½ cup (3 oz/90 g) whole blanched almonds or ¾ cup (3 oz/90 g) purchased ground almonds

½ cup (4 fl oz/120 ml) milk

½ cup (4 fl oz/120 ml) heavy (double) cream

⅓ cup (3 oz/90 g) plus 1 tablespoon sugar

2 eggs

½ vanilla bean, split lengthwise

1 tablespoon unsalted butter

¾ cup (3 oz/90 g) peeled, cored and diced firm green apple

1 mango, peeled, pitted and diced

½ cup (2 oz/60 g) blackberries

Confectioners' (icing) sugar (optional), for dusting

124

Preheat an oven to 400°F (200°C/Gas Mark 5).

If you are using whole almonds, place the nuts in a nut grinder or in a food processor fitted with a metal blade. Grind or process until the nuts are a fine powder. (Do not overprocess.)

In a large bowl, combine the milk, cream, ground almonds, the ⅓ cup (3 oz/90 g) sugar and the eggs. Using the tip of a knife, scrape the seeds from the vanilla bean directly into the bowl. Using a wire whisk, mix until well combined; set aside.

In a sauté pan over medium heat, melt the butter. Add the apple and the 1 tablespoon sugar and sauté, stirring, until lightly caramelized, 3–4 minutes. Remove from the heat.

Scatter the apple, mango and blackberries in the bottom of 4 round gratin dishes 5½ inches (14 cm) in diameter. Pour the milk mixture over the fruit.

Bake until the pudding is set and a knife inserted into the center of the dish comes out clean, 20–25 minutes.

Transfer to a rack and let cool for at least 30 minutes before serving warm. Dust with the confectioners' sugar, if desired.

Makes 4

Fruit

Sautéed Figs with Roasted Almonds and Cream Mousseline

Sugar-roasted almonds (page 29)

CREAM MOUSSELINE

½ cup (4 fl oz/120 ml) crème anglaise (page 28)

1 cup (8 fl oz/240 ml) heavy (double) cream

FIGS

2 tablespoons unsalted butter

12 ripe Black Mission figs, cut lengthwise into halves

2½ tablespoons firmly packed brown sugar

Confectioners' (icing) sugar

Prepare the sugar-roasted almonds as directed. Set aside.

For the cream mousseline, prepare the crème anglaise and set aside. Pour the heavy cream into a large bowl and whisk vigorously until it forms soft peaks. Add the crème anglaise and whisk until combined.

For the figs, in a large sauté pan over high heat, melt the butter. As soon as the butter starts to sizzle, add the fig halves and sprinkle with the brown sugar. Sauté, turning the figs gently, until they begin to turn golden brown, 3–5 minutes. Remove from the heat.

Spoon the heavy cream mixture into 4 shallow serving bowls, dividing it equally. Then spoon an equal amount of the figs into the center of each bowl.

Sprinkle evenly with about ⅔ cup (3 oz/90 g) of the sugar-roasted almonds; reserve the remaining almonds for another use. Then sprinkle lightly with confectioners' sugar and serve immediately.

Serves 4

Strawberry Shortcakes

SHORTCAKES

2 cups (10 oz/300 g) all-purpose (plain) flour

2 tablespoons sugar

2 teaspoons baking powder

½ teaspoon salt

2 tablespoons chilled butter, cut into pieces

1½ teaspoons grated lemon zest (rind)

¾ cup (6 fl oz/180 ml) heavy (double) cream

¼ cup (2 fl oz/60 ml) milk

2 tablespoons butter, at room temperature

FILLING

2 cups (8 oz/240 g) strawberries, hulled and chopped

¼ cup (2 oz/60 g) sugar

1 teaspoon lemon juice

1 cup (8 fl oz/240 ml) heavy (double) cream, whipped

Extra strawberries, halved, to garnish

Preheat an oven to 400°F (200°C/Gas Mark 5). Butter a baking sheet.

For the shortcakes, in a large bowl, sift together the flour, sugar, baking powder and salt. Add the butter and lemon zest and, using your fingertips, rub into the flour until the mixture resembles coarse crumbs. Stir in cream to make a soft dough.

On a floured surface, quickly form the dough into a ball. Roll or pat it out to ½ inch (1 cm) thick. Cut out 3-inch (7.5-cm) rounds and arrange them on the baking sheet. Form scraps gently into a ball, roll it out and cut more rounds. Brush the tops of the rounds lightly with the milk. Bake until puffed and golden, 15–20 minutes.

Split cakes horizontally with a knife. While still warm, spread the halves with the butter.

For the filling, combine the strawberries, sugar and lemon juice in a small saucepan over moderate heat. Bring to a boil, then cook, stirring constantly, for 5 minutes. Transfer to a bowl and cool completely.

Cover the bottom half of each cake with the strawberry filling and some of the cream. Add the top halves of the cakes and more cream, and decorate each cake with a half-strawberry. Serve immediately.

Makes 8

French Apple Tart

Sweet Pastry Dough (page 20)

5 tart green apples, such as Granny Smith

1 cup (8 fl oz/240 ml) pastry cream (page 27), cooled

2 tablespoons unsalted butter, melted

1 tablespoon sugar

Heavy (double) cream (optional), to serve

Prepare pastry as directed. On a lightly floured work surface, roll out the dough into a round 12 inches (30 cm) in diameter and ⅛ inch (3 mm) thick. Drape the dough over a rolling pin and transfer it to a 10-inch (25-cm) tart pan with a removable bottom. Unwrap the dough from the pin and press it gently into the pan. Trim the pastry even with the pan rim and place in the refrigerator.

Preheat an oven to 375°F (190°C/Gas Mark 4).

Peel the apples, then halve them and core them. Slice the apples lengthwise as thinly as possible.

Remove the pastry shell from the refrigerator and spread it with the cooled pastry cream. It should be ⅛ inch (3 mm) deep. Arrange the apple slices on top of the pastry cream in concentric circles. Brush the apple slices with the melted butter, coating them evenly, then sprinkle with the sugar.

Bake in the oven until golden brown and slightly caramelized, about 50 minutes.

Transfer to a rack and remove the pan sides. Serve warm or at room temperature with cream, if desired.

Serves 6 to 8

131

Poached Autumn Pears with Mascarpone and Ginger

POACHED PEARS

2 large ripe pears

1½ cups (12 fl oz/360 ml) sweet dessert wine

1 stick cinnamon, 3 inches (7.5 cm) long, broken in half

½ teaspoon allspice berries or 1 whole clove

TOPPING

½ cup (4 oz/120 g) mascarpone cheese

2 teaspoons confectioners' (icing) sugar, or to taste

1 teaspoon milk

2 teaspoons chopped candied (glacéed) ginger

4 fresh mint sprigs (optional), to garnish

For the pears, cut the pears in half lengthwise, then core and peel the halves. In a saucepan, combine the sweet dessert wine, cinnamon and allspice berries or the clove and bring to a boil.

Place the pears in the liquid, cored side down, reduce the heat to medium-low and simmer for 4–5 minutes. Turn the pears

over and poach until barely soft when pierced with a sharp knife, 4–5 minutes longer. Using a slotted spoon, carefully place each pear half, cored side down, in the center of an individual serving plate.

Reduce the poaching liquid over medium heat until it forms a thick syrup, about 5 minutes. Strain through a fine-mesh sieve into a clean container. Discard the contents of the sieve.

For the topping, in a bowl, whisk together the mascarpone, sugar and milk until smooth.

To serve, cut each pear half into a fan shape: hold a paring knife at a 45-degree angle to the pear, and make slashes completely through it, but leave the top intact. Gently press on the slices to spread them out and then drizzle the reduced syrup over the top. Put a dollop of the mascarpone mixture at the top of each pear. Sprinkle evenly with the candied ginger and garnish with the mint sprigs, if desired.

Serves 4

Fresh Peach Tart

FILLING

3½ lb (1.6 kg) ripe but firm yellow peaches, peeled, pitted and chopped

½ cup (4 oz/120 g) sugar or ⅓ cup (4 oz/120 g) honey, or to taste

1 tablespoon cornstarch (cornflour)

PASTRY

¼ cup (1 oz/30 g) slivered, blanched almonds

½ cup (4 oz/120 g) sugar

2 cups (10 oz/300 g) all-purpose (plain) flour

Pinch of baking soda (bicarbonate of soda)

Pinch of salt

2 extra-large eggs

2 teaspoons vanilla extract (essence)

1 teaspoon finely grated lemon zest (rind)

1 teaspoon finely grated orange zest (rind)

⅓ cup (2½ fl oz/75 ml) mild-flavored olive oil

1 teaspoon white vinegar

For the filling, toss the peaches in a bowl with the sugar or honey; let stand for 1 hour. Drain, reserving the liquid for another purpose, and let cool.

Preheat an oven to 425°F (210°C/Gas Mark 5).

For the pastry, combine the almonds and a little of the sugar in a food processor fitted with a metal blade and process until finely ground.

Add the remaining sugar, the flour, baking soda and salt, and pulse briefly until blended.

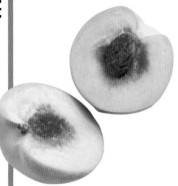

Whisk the eggs in a small bowl with the vanilla, lemon zest and orange zest; set aside. Turn the food processor on and pour in the oil, then the vinegar and finally the egg mixture, mixing for only a few seconds until a ball of dough forms. Divide the dough into 2 portions, one twice as large as the other. Cover and refrigerate the smaller portion.

Place the large dough portion between 2 sheets of floured waxed (greaseproof) paper. Roll into a round about 11 inches (28 cm) in diameter and ⅛ inch (3 mm) thick. Peel off 1 piece of paper and transfer, paper-side up, to a 9-inch (23-cm) round tart pan with a removable base. Remove paper and press pastry into pan; trim off the overhang. Stir cornstarch into the filling mixture and spoon into pastry.

Roll out the remaining dough portion to a 10-inch (25-cm) round. Using a pastry wheel, cut into strips ½ inch (1 cm) wide. Make a decorative lattice with the strips, trimming off any overhang, and pressing the strips against the rim to secure them. (See page 170 for woven lattice.)

Reduce the oven heat to 375°F (190°C/Gas Mark 4) and bake the tart for 25–30 minutes on a baking sheet in the center of the oven. Rotate the tart to ensure even browning and reduce heat to 300°F (150°C/Gas Mark 2).

Bake for 20–25 minutes longer, or until the crust is golden brown. Serve cool.

Serves 8 to 10

Plum Cake

⅓ cup (3 oz/90 g) unsalted butter, at room temperature

⅓ cup (3 oz/90 g), plus 1 teaspoon, granulated sugar

2 extra-large eggs, separated, at room temperature

1 cup (5 oz/150 g) unbleached all-purpose (plain) flour

2½ teaspoons baking powder

¼ cup (2 fl oz/60 ml) water

¼ cup (2 fl oz/60 ml) heavy (double) cream

2 teaspoons almond extract (essence)

1½ teaspoons vanilla extract (essence)

2 ripe plums, peeled, pitted and sliced into sixths

Confectioners' (icing) sugar for dusting

Preheat an oven to 400°F (200°C/Gas Mark 5). Butter and flour a 9-inch (23-cm) round cake pan or a tart pan with a removable bottom.

In a bowl, using an electric mixer on medium speed, beat together the butter and the ⅓ cup (3 oz/90 g) granulated sugar until smooth and fluffy, 2–3 minutes. Add the egg yolks and beat until very smooth.

In a small bowl, stir together the flour and baking powder. In another small bowl, combine the water, cream and almond and vanilla extracts. Stir the flour mixture into the butter mixture alternately with the cream mixture, beginning and ending with the flour mixture. Do not overmix.

In a clean bowl, using clean beaters, whip the egg whites until they form semisoft peaks. Sprinkle in the 1 teaspoon granulated sugar and continue to beat until soft peaks form. Using a rubber spatula or whisk, fold the beaten egg whites into the batter, breaking apart any lumps. Pour the batter into the prepared pan and level the surface.

Arrange the plums in a circle on the top of the batter. Place in the center of the oven and immediately reduce the heat to 350°F (180°C/Gas Mark 4). Bake until the cake pulls away from the sides of the pan and

a wooden skewer inserted into the center of the cake comes out clean, 35–40 minutes. Transfer to a rack and let cool slightly.

If using a cake pan, run a knife blade around the edge of the pan to loosen the cake, invert onto the rack and then turn the cake right side up. If using a tart pan, remove the pan sides.

Place the cake on a serving plate and using a fine-mesh sieve, sift confectioners' sugar evenly over the top. Serve warm or at room temperature.

Serves 8

Lemon Tart

Sweet Pastry Dough (page 20)

4 lemons

4 eggs

1¾ cups (14 oz/420 g) sugar

⅓ cup (3 fl oz/90 ml) unsalted butter, melted

½ cup (4 fl oz/120 ml) water

Preheat an oven to 400°F (200°C/Gas Mark 5). Butter the bottom and the sides of a 10-inch (25-cm) tart pan that has a removable bottom.

On a lightly floured work surface, roll out the dough into a round 12 inches (30 cm) in diameter and ⅛ inch (3 mm) thick. Press the pastry gently into the pan and trim even with the pan rim.

Line the pastry-lined pan with waxed (greaseproof) paper and add pie weights or dried beans. Bake until the pie pastry is half-cooked, about 15 minutes.

Meanwhile, cut 3 paper-thin slices from the center of 1 of the lemons and set aside. Grate the zest (rind) from the lemon halves and the remaining lemons into a bowl. Cut the whole lemons in half and squeeze the juice from the halves through a fine-mesh sieve into a measuring cup; you should have about ½ cup (4 fl oz/120 ml) juice.

Add the lemon juice and eggs to the zest and whisk until well combined. Add 1¼ cups (10 oz/300 g) of the sugar and mix until well combined. Stir in the melted butter until combined.

As soon as the crust is half-cooked, remove it from the oven and immediately remove the pie weights and waxed paper. Pour the citrus mixture into the warm tart shell and return it to the oven. Bake until the filling is set and the edges are golden brown, about 20 minutes.

Meanwhile, in a small saucepan set over a medium-high heat, combine the remaining ½ cup (4 oz/120 g) sugar and water.

Bring to a boil, stirring constantly to dissolve the sugar. Add the reserved lemon slices, reduce the heat to low, and simmer until tender, about 10 minutes. Remove the pan from the heat and set aside. When the tart is done, transfer it to a rack and remove the pan sides. Allow to cool completely.

Remove the lemon slices from the sugar and water mixture, shaking briefly to remove any excess liquid, and arrange them in an overlapping pattern on the center of the tart. Transfer the tart to a serving plate and serve at room temperature.

Serves 6

Fruit

Melon Sorbet

¼ cup (2 fl oz/60 ml) water

¼ cup (2 oz/60 g), plus
1 teaspoon, sugar

2½ lb (1.2 kg) cantaloupes

2 extra-large egg whites

In a deep saucepan, combine the water and the ¼ cup (2 oz/60 g) sugar and bring to a boil over high heat. Be careful not to stir the mixture or it will crystallize. Continue to boil the syrup until it becomes thick and clear, about 5 minutes. Remove from the heat and let cool.

Cut the cantaloupes in half, then remove and discard the seeds. Cut off and discard the rind. Chop the melon pulp coarsely; you should have about 1½ lb (720 g) pulp.

Working in batches if necessary, place the melon pulp in a food processor or in a blender and purée until smooth. Transfer the puréed melon to a bowl, add the cooled syrup and stir until blended. Cover and chill well, at least 2 hours.

Transfer the melon mixture to an ice-cream maker and freeze according to the manufacturer's instructions.

Meanwhile, using a clean bowl and an electric mixer on high speed, beat the egg whites until frothy. Add the 1 teaspoon sugar and then continue to beat until semisoft peaks form.

When the melon mixture is slushy and a little frozen, add the egg whites to the mixture and then continue to freeze until solid.

To serve, spoon into bowls and serve immediately.

Serves 4

Apple Crisp with Dried Cranberries

TOPPING

1 cup (4 oz/120 g) coarsely chopped pecans

¾ cup (4 oz/120 g) all-purpose (plain) flour

½ teaspoon ground cinnamon

¼ teaspoon ground nutmeg

¼ teaspoon ground allspice

⅛ teaspoon ground cloves

Pinch of salt

¾ cup (2½ oz/75 g) quick-cooking rolled oats

½ cup (4 oz/120 g) granulated sugar

½ cup (3½ oz/105 g) firmly packed light brown sugar

¾ cup (6 oz/180 g) unsalted butter, chilled, cut into pieces

FILLING

8 apples, about 2½ lb (1.2 kg) total weight

3 tablespoons fresh lemon juice

½ cup (2 oz/60 g) dried cranberries

Ice cream (optional), to serve

Preheat an oven to 350°F (180°C/Gas Mark 4). Butter a 9- x 12-inch (23- x 30-cm) oval baking dish.

For the topping, spread the pecans on a baking sheet and bake until lightly toasted, about 5 minutes. Remove from the oven and let cool.

In a large bowl, stir together the flour, cinnamon, nutmeg, allspice, cloves and salt. Add the toasted pecans, rolled oats, granulated sugar, brown sugar and butter. Using your fingers, rub the mixture together until it resembles coarse crumbs. Set aside.

For the filling, peel, halve and core the apples, then cut lengthwise into slices ½ inch (1 cm) thick. Place in a bowl, immediately add the lemon juice and dried cranberries and toss

to coat with the juice. Pour the filling into the prepared dish, leveling the surface. Sprinkle the topping evenly over the fruit, pressing down on it lightly and leaving about ¼ inch (5 mm) space between the topping and the pan sides.

Bake for 40–45 minutes until the topping is golden brown and bubbling. Cover the top with aluminum foil if the crust begins to overbrown.

Transfer to a rack and let cool for 15 minutes before serving with ice cream, if desired.

Serves 6

Port Wine Jelly

2½ cups (20 fl oz/600 ml) water

½ cup (4 oz/120 g) sugar

2 tablespoons redcurrant jelly

2 tablespoons (2 envelopes) gelatin

10 fl oz (300 ml) port wine

Place the water, sugar and redcurrant jelly in a saucepan. Stir over a low heat until the sugar and jelly dissolve.

In a bowl, dissolve the gelatin in 2 tablespoons of cold water set over hot water. Add the gelatin to the redcurrant jelly mixture. Stir in the port, pour into a large decorative mold and refrigerate until set.

Serves 8

Dried Fruit Compote

1 cup (6 oz/180 g) whole pitted prunes

1 cup (6 oz/180 g) whole dried apricot halves

1 cup (3 oz/90 g) dried apple rings

½ cup (3 oz/90 g) raisins

½ cup (4 oz/120 g) superfine (caster) sugar

1½ cups (12 fl oz/360 ml) white wine

1 cup (8 fl oz/240 ml) water

Lemon zest (rind), in thick strips

2 whole cloves

½ teaspoon ground allspice

Heavy (double) cream, whipped (optional), to serve

Toasted flaked almonds (optional), to serve

Place all of the fruit into a slow cooker or a large, heavy saucepan and sprinkle with the sugar. Pour on the white wine and water. Add the lemon zest, whole cloves and allspice.

Put on the lid and cook on low for 3–4 hours. The fruit should be soft but not mushy. Remove the lemon zest and whole cloves.

Serve warm or cold. Top with the whipped cream and sprinkle with the toasted flaked almonds, if desired.

Serves 4 to 6

Lemon Meringue Pie

Tart Pastry (page 17)

FILLING

1 cup (8 oz/240 g) sugar

⅓ cup (1½ oz/45 g) cornstarch (cornflour)

¼ teaspoon salt

2 cups (16 fl oz/480 ml) water

4 well-beaten egg yolks

3 tablespoons unsalted butter

½ cup (4 fl oz/120 ml) strained fresh lemon juice

Finely grated zest (rind) of 1 large lemon

MERINGUE

5 egg whites

¼ teaspoon cream of tartar

⅛ teaspoon salt

½ cup (4 oz/120 g) sugar

Prepare and bake the tart pastry as directed and let cool.

Preheat an oven to 350°F (180°C/Gas Mark 4).

For the filling, in a heavy non-aluminum saucepan, combine the sugar, cornstarch and salt and whisk until smooth. Stir in the water, a few drops at a time at first and then in greater amounts, adding more water gradually until mixture is smooth. Stir in the yolks, whisking well to combine.

Place the saucepan over medium heat and bring to a boil, stirring constantly with a wooden spoon over the bottom and to the edge of the pan. Switch to a whisk occasionally to prevent lumps from forming.

When the mixture reaches a boil, 7–8 minutes, boil for 1 minute, stirring constantly. Remove the pan from the heat, add the butter and gradually stir in the lemon juice, only a few drops at a time at first, until incorporated and the butter is melted. Stir in the lemon zest. Pour the hot filling into the cooled pie crust, then make the meringue immediately.

For the meringue, in a large, clean bowl, using an electric mixer on medium speed, beat the egg whites for a few seconds to break them up.

Add the cream of tartar and salt and continue beating until soft peaks form, about 2 minutes. Increase the speed to high and add the sugar in a slow, steady stream, stopping occasionally to scrape down the sides of the bowl. Continue beating until stiff peaks form, 2–3 minutes.

Spoon about one-fourth of the meringue onto the top of the hot filling and spread it to meet the crust. Place the remaining meringue in the center of the pie and, using the back of a spoon, shape and spread the meringue into peaks. Bake until the meringue is golden brown and firm to the touch, rotating a few times to promote even coloring, about 15 minutes. Transfer to a rack and let cool completely.

Serve at room temperature or store in the refrigerator for up to 1 day, uncovered. Bring to room temperature before serving.

Serves 6 to 8

Banana Split

½ cup (2½ oz/75 g) slivered blanched almonds

FUDGE SAUCE

4 oz (120 g) bittersweet (plain) chocolate, coarsely chopped

¼ cup (2 oz/60 g) unsalted butter

¼ cup (2 fl oz/60 ml) heavy (double) cream

CARAMEL SAUCE

½ cup (4 fl oz/120 ml) heavy (double) cream

½ cup (3½ oz/105 g) firmly packed light or dark brown sugar

1 tablespoon unsalted butter

4 ripe bananas

4 scoops vanilla ice cream

4 scoops chocolate ice cream

4 scoops strawberry ice cream

1 cup (8 fl oz/240 ml) heavy (double) cream, whipped to soft peaks and chilled

4 maraschino cherries

BANANA SPLIT

Preheat an oven to 350°F (180°C/Gas Mark 4). Spread the almonds on a baking sheet and bake until lightly toasted, about 5 minutes. Remove from the oven and let cool.

For the fudge sauce, in the top pan of a double boiler or in a heatproof bowl set over (not touching) simmering water in a pan, combine the chocolate and butter and stir until melted and smooth. Stir in the ¼ cup (2 fl oz/60 ml) cream just until incorporated. Remove the pan from the heat, cover to keep warm and set aside.

For the caramel sauce, in a heavy saucepan over medium-high heat, stir together the ½ cup (4 fl oz/120 ml) cream and brown sugar and bring to a boil. Boil for 2 minutes, stirring constantly.

Add the butter, reduce the heat to low and simmer until thick and caramel-like, about 2 minutes. Remove from the heat, cover to keep warm and set aside.

Peel the bananas and cut in half lengthwise. Lay each banana on an individual serving plate, cut side up. Arrange 1 scoop each of vanilla, chocolate and strawberry ice cream on each banana.

Drizzle a little warm fudge sauce over the chocolate and over the strawberry ice cream and a little warm caramel sauce over the vanilla ice cream.

Top with a mound of whipped cream and then sprinkle with the toasted almonds. Finally, crown with a maraschino cherry and serve immediately. Serve the remaining fudge and caramel sauces on the side.

Serves 4

Strawberry and Rhubarb Pie

Pastry for double-crust pie
(page 12)

1¼ cups (10 oz/300 g)
granulated sugar

3 tablespoons quick-cooking
tapioca

3 cups (12 oz/360 g)
strawberries, sliced

2 cups (8 oz/240 g) fresh or
thawed frozen unsweetened
sliced rhubarb

½ teaspoon finely shredded
orange zest (rind)

½ teaspoon ground cinnamon

¼ teaspoon ground nutmeg

¼ cup (2 oz/60 g) superfine
(caster) sugar

Prepare the pastry as directed
and set aside to rest.

Preheat an oven to 375°F
(190°C/Gas Mark 4).

Combine the granulated sugar
and the tapioca in a large bowl.
Add the strawberries, rhubarb,
orange zest, cinnamon and
nutmeg. Toss until the fruit
is coated, then stand, stirring
occasionally, for 12–15 minutes,
or until a syrup forms.

Divide the pastry into halves
and roll out. Line a 9-inch
(23-cm) pie plate with half the
pastry. Stir the fruit mixture and

transfer to pastry-lined pie plate.
Place the remaining crust over
the filling. Seal and crimp the
edge and trim off even with rim.
Cut slits in the top crust, brush
with water and sprinkle with
the superfine sugar. To prevent
overbrowning, cover the edge
of the pie with aluminum foil.

Bake for 25 minutes. Remove
the foil and bake for another
20–25 minutes, or until the top
is golden. Cool on a wire rack.

Serves 8

Raisin and Citrus Peel Pies

PASTRY

2 cups (8 oz/240 g) sifted
all-purpose (plain) flour

½ teaspoon salt

¾ cup (6 oz/180 g)
cold unsalted butter

⅓ cup (2½ fl oz/75 ml)
cold water

1 beaten egg

FILLING

½ cup (3 oz/90 g) chopped
raisins

¼ cup (1⅓ oz/40 g) mixed
candied (glacéed) citrus peel

2 tablespoons honey

¼ cup (2 oz/60 g) unsalted
butter, melted

¼ cup (2 oz/60 g) firmly packed
dark brown sugar

Whipped cream, flavored with
1 teaspoon ground allspice,
to serve

For the pastry, mix together the
flour and salt. Rub in the butter
until the mixture resembles
coarse breadcrumbs. Slowly add
the water, a tablespoon at a time,
mixing with your fingertips,
until the pastry comes together.
Press gently into a ball. Wrap
in plastic wrap and refrigerate
for 30 minutes.

For the filling, mix together the
raisins, citrus peel, honey, butter
and dark brown sugar.

Preheat an oven to 400°F
(200°C/Gas Mark 6). Lightly
grease a large baking sheet.

Roll out the pie pastry to a
thickness of ⅓ inch (8 mm).
Cut out thirty-six 2-inch (5-cm)
rounds. Do this in batches,
keeping the prepared circles
under a clean dish towel to
prevent the pastry drying out.

Place 1 teaspoon of the filling
in the center of 18 of the pastry
rounds. Moisten the edges with
a little milk or beaten egg and

place a round of the pastry over
each filled round. Seal the edges
firmly with the tines of a fork
and cut a small cross-shaped
incision in the top of each pie.

Bake the pies for 10–15 minutes,
or until golden brown.

Serve warm with the whipped
cream flavored with the allspice.

Makes 18

Blueberry Hotcakes

2 cups (10 oz/300 g) all-purpose (plain) flour

2 teaspoons baking powder

1 teaspoon baking soda (bicarbonate of soda)

⅓ cup (2½ oz/75 g) superfine (caster) sugar

2 eggs

1¼ cups (10 fl oz/300 ml) milk

⅓ cup (3 oz/90 g) butter, melted

2 cups (8 oz/240 g) fresh blueberries

Extra butter, for greasing

Crème fraîche, heavy (double) cream or maple syrup, to serve

In a large bowl, sift together the flour, baking powder and baking soda. Stir through the superfine sugar. Make a well in the center.

In a small bowl, whisk together the eggs, milk and melted butter. Add all at once to the flour. Whisk just until all the ingredients are combined and no lumps remain. Thin with a little extra milk if the batter is too thick. Gently fold in the blueberries.

Grease a nonstick frying pan with butter. Over a low heat, warm the pan. When hot, add ½ cup (4 fl oz/120 ml) of the batter. Using a spatula, spread evenly into a pancake about 6 inches (15 cm) across. Cook until bubbles appear on the surface. Turn and cook a further 2–3 minutes. Keep warm in a low oven while cooking the rest of the batter in the same way.

Serve warm with crème fraîche, heavy cream or maple syrup.

Makes 6

Pear and Nut Tart

PASTRY

1 cup (5 oz/150 g) roasted hazelnuts, skins removed

½ cup (2½ oz/75 g) all-purpose (plain) flour

1 tablespoon firmly packed brown sugar

2 tablespoons (1 oz/30 g) unsalted butter, melted

1 egg yolk

FILLING

10 oz (300 g) mascarpone cheese

1 can (28 oz/840 g) pear halves, drained

2 oz (60 g) semisweet (plain) chocolate, melted

Preheat an oven to 350°F (180°C/Gas Mark 4).

For the pastry, place the roasted hazelnuts in a food processor and process until fine. Add the flour and sugar and process to combine. Add the butter and the egg yolk and process until the mixture forms a mass. Do not overprocess. Press the pastry into an 8-inch (20-cm) round springform pan. Prick the pan bottom with the tines of a fork.

Bake for 25 minutes, or until the pastry is golden. Remove from the oven and allow to cool.

For the filling, when the pastry shell has cooled, fill with the mascarpone and top with the pears. Drizzle with the melted chocolate.

Serves 4

Rhubarb and Sour Cream Cake

¼ cup (2 oz/60 g) unsalted butter, at room temperature

1¼ cups (9 oz/270 g) firmly packed brown sugar

1 egg, slightly beaten

1 teaspoon vanilla extract (essence)

1½ cups (7½ oz/225 g) all-purpose (plain) flour, sifted

1 teaspoon baking powder

1 cup (8 fl oz/240 ml) sour cream

4 cups (15 oz/450 g) sliced rhubarb (½-inch/1-cm pieces)

⅓ cup (2½ oz/75 g) superfine (caster) sugar

½ teaspoon freshly grated nutmeg

Heavy (double) cream (optional), to serve

Preheat an oven to 375°F (190°C/Gas Mark 4). Butter an 8- x 10-inch (20- x 25-cm) loaf pan and line with parchment (baking) paper.

Cream the butter and sugar until fluffy, about 3–4 minutes.

Beat in the egg and vanilla. Fold in the flour and baking powder alternately with the sour cream and rhubarb. Pour the mixture into the prepared pan. Combine the sugar and nutmeg and then sprinkle over the cake mixture.

Bake for 40 minutes, or until a wooden skewer inserted in the middle of the cake comes out clean. Allow the cake to cool in the pan for 30 minutes before turning out. Serve warm with heavy cream, if desired.

Serves 10 to 12

Citrus Roulade

LEMON CURD

½ cup (4 oz/120 g) unsalted butter

⅔ cup (3 fl oz/90 ml) lemon juice

1¼ cups (10 oz/300 g) granulated sugar

3 whole eggs

3 egg yolks

CAKE

4 eggs

½ cup (4 oz/120 g) granulated sugar

¾ cup (3 oz/90 g) all-purpose (plain) flour, sifted

½ teaspoon baking powder

1 teaspoon grated lemon zest (rind)

1 teaspoon vanilla extract (essence)

½ cup (2 oz/60 g) confectioners' (icing) sugar, to garnish

For the lemon curd, combine butter, lemon juice and 1¼ cups (10 oz/300 g) granulated sugar in the top of a double boiler or in a heatproof bowl set over (not touching) simmering water in a pan. Stir until butter melts and sugar dissolves. Whisk together the whole eggs and egg yolks in a bowl. Slowly add one-quarter of the hot lemon mixture while whisking, then add the rest in a steady stream. Return to the top pan of the double boiler or

heatproof bowl over a pan and cook, stirring, until thick. Cover and refrigerate for 12 hours.

Preheat an oven to 350°F (180°C/Gas Mark 4). Line a jelly roll pan (jam roll tin) with parchment (baking) paper and butter the paper.

For the cake, in the top pan of a double boiler or in a heatproof bowl, whisk together the eggs and the ½ cup (4 oz/120 g) granulated sugar until blended. Set over simmering water and heat, stirring, until warm to touch. Remove from heat and beat with electric mixer until doubled in volume and pale yellow in color. Fold in flour, baking powder, lemon zest and vanilla. Pour into prepared pan and bake for 13–15 minutes, or until springy to touch. Run a knife around the cake and invert onto a damp tea towel. Roll up starting with short edge. Do not roll up tea towel.

To assemble, unroll the cake, spread with lemon curd, re-roll and place, seam side down, on a plate. Dust the top and sides with sifted confectioners' sugar.

Serves 8

Apple Brioche Cake

1 cup (8 oz/240 g) unsalted butter

4 lb (1.9 kg) green apples, peeled, cored and cut into 1-inch (2.5-cm) cubes

2 tablespoons lemon juice

1 vanilla bean, split lengthwise

¾ cup (6 oz/180 g) sugar

3 tablespoons Calvados or brandy

2 (1¾ lb/840 g) brioche loaves, cut into slices ½-inch (1-cm) thick with crusts removed

Heavy (double) cream, to serve

Melt ½ cup (4 oz/120 g) butter in a large saucepan. Add the apples, lemon juice, vanilla bean, sugar and Calvados or brandy. Cook over a medium-low heat for 35 minutes or until the apples are soft and most of the liquid is absorbed. Remove from the heat and discard the vanilla bean. Allow to cool.

Preheat an oven to 400°F (200°C/Gas Mark 5). Butter a 6-inch (15-cm) charlotte mold.

Melt the remaining ½ cup (4 oz/120 g) butter in a small saucepan.

Fan 6–7 slices of brioche evenly in a full circle on a work surface. Place the charlotte mold on top and trim the brioche to the edge of the base with a serrated knife. Butter both sides of each slice of brioche. Reserving 4 slices of brioche for the top, line the mold with the brioche slices, overlapping the edges slightly. Fill with the apple mixture and top with the remaining brioche slices. Chill in the refrigerator.

Remove the cake from the refrigerator after 15 minutes, then bake for 30–40 minutes, or until the brioche on top is golden. Allow to cool for at least 30 minutes, then slice the cake into wedges and serve with heavy cream.

Serves 10

Cherry-Berry Lattice Pie

Pastry for double-crust pie
(page 12)

1–1¼ cups (8–10 oz/250–315 g)
sugar, to taste

⅓ cup (2 oz/60 g) all-purpose
(plain) flour

3 cups (12 oz/360 g) raspberries

2 cups (10 oz/300 g) pitted,
tart red cherries

¼ teaspoon almond extract
(essence)

Preheat an oven to 375°F
(190°C/Gas Mark 4).

Prepare and roll out pastry as
directed. Line a 9-inch (23-cm)
pie plate with half of the pastry.

In a large bowl, combine sugar
and flour. Add raspberries,
cherries and almond extract.
Toss gently till fruit is coated.

Stir filling and transfer to the
pastry-lined pie plate. Trim the
pastry to ½ inch (1 cm) beyond
the edge of the pie plate.

For the woven lattice, cut the
other half of the rolled pastry
into ½-inch-wide (1-cm-wide)
strips. Lay one long strip of
lattice across the center of the
pie filling. Set a second strip
perpendicular to the first. Then
add two more strips, one on
either side of the first. Fold back
the middle strip. Lay another
strip underneath it and over the

two remaining strips. Unfold the
folded strip. Repeat on the other
side. Fold back the two strips
that are under the perpendicular
strip; lay another strip across
and unfold the folded strips.
Repeat in each direction from
the center. Do not stretch the
strips or they will shrink.

Trim the strips even with the
edge of the bottom crust. Seal
and crimp the edge of the pastry.
To prevent overbrowning, cover
the pie edge with aluminum foil.

Bake for 25 minutes. Remove
foil and bake for 20–25 minutes
more or until the top is golden.

Serves 8

Summer Puddings

PUDDINGS

16 slices stale white bread, crusts removed

½ cup (4 oz/120 g) blueberries

½ cup (4 oz/120 g) raspberries

⅓ cup (3 oz/90 g) sugar

½ cup (4 oz/120 g) strawberries, chopped

Whipped cream and extra berries (optional), to serve

STRAWBERRY SAUCE

1 cup (8 oz/240 g) strawberries

3 tablespoons sugar

1 tablespoon water

For the puddings, line four 6-ounce (9-cm) round molds or ramekins with bread, making sure there is no space between the pieces. Cut a "lid" for each from some of the bread.

Place the blueberries and raspberries in a saucepan with ⅓ cup (3 oz/90 g) sugar and cook on low heat, 3–4 minutes, stirring gently. Then add the chopped strawberries and cook for 1 minute.

Pour the fruit into the prepared molds and place a lid over each. Cover with plastic wrap and set a weight on the top of each pudding. Refrigerate overnight.

For the strawberry sauce, place the whole strawberries into a saucepan with 3 tablespoons sugar and the water. Cook over low heat to dissolve the sugar.

Bring to a boil and simmer for 3 minutes or until strawberries are completely soft. Place in a food processor and purée. Strain through a fine sieve. Discard the contents of the sieve.

Unmold the puddings and drizzle with the strawberry sauce. Serve with whipped cream and berries, if desired.

Makes 4

Tangerine Sorbet

2 tablespoons grated tangerine zest (rind)

3½ cups (28 fl oz/840 ml) fresh tangerine juice (18–20 tangerines)

½ cup (4 fl oz/120 ml) fresh lemon juice (3–4 lemons)

1¼ cups (10 oz/300 g) sugar

¼ cup (2½ fl oz/75 ml) light corn syrup

Shredded tangerine zest (optional), to garnish

In a large bowl, combine the tangerine zest and juice, lemon juice, sugar and corn syrup. Stir until the sugar dissolves. Transfer to an ice-cream maker and freeze according to the manufacturer's instructions. Pack into a freezer container and place in the freezer until set, 2–4 hours.

Garnish with tangerine zest, if desired. Serve immediately.

Serves 6 to 8

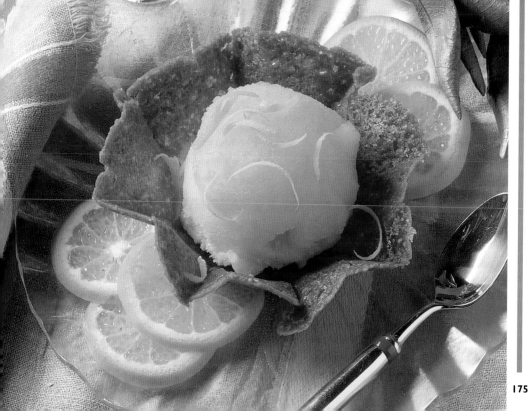

Spiced Baked Apples

¼ cup (1 oz/30 g) pecan halves

⅓ cup (3 oz/90 g) unsalted butter, chilled, cut into small pieces

⅓ cup (2½ oz/75 g) firmly packed light or dark brown sugar

2 tablespoons coarsely chopped dried apricots

2 tablespoons golden raisins (sultanas)

½ teaspoon ground cinnamon

⅛ teaspoon ground cloves

¼ teaspoon ground allspice

⅛ teaspoon ground nutmeg

6 baking apples, such as Rome Beauty

1 cup (8 fl oz/240 ml) apple juice

Preheat an oven to 350°F (180°C/Gas Mark 4). Spread the pecan halves on a baking sheet and bake until lightly toasted, 5–7 minutes. Remove from the oven, let cool and chop coarsely. Set aside. Increase the oven temperature to 400°F (200°C/ Gas Mark 5).

In a small bowl, combine the butter and sugar. Mix to a paste-like consistency, then stir in the toasted pecans, apricots, raisins, cinnamon, cloves, allspice and nutmeg. Set aside.

Cut a thin slice off the bottom of each apple so that it will stand upright. Working from the stem ends and using a sharp knife, core the apples without piercing the bottoms.

Using a small spoon, stuff the mixture into the cored apples, dividing it equally. Smooth the tops and cover just the filling with aluminum foil.

Place apples in a 9- x 13-inch (23- x 33-cm) baking dish. Pour the apple juice into the baking dish. Bake, basting with the dish juices every 15 minutes, until tender when pierced with a knife, 45–60 minutes.

Transfer the baked apples to a platter or individual serving dishes and serve immediately.

Serves 6

Lime and Mango Mousse with Passionfruit Sauce

MOUSSE

3 limes

¾ cup (6 oz/180 g) sugar

1 cup (8 fl oz/240 ml) water

4 tablespoons (4 envelopes) gelatin

6 large ripe mangoes, peeled, pitted and coarsely chopped

5 oz (150 g) ricotta or mascarpone cheese

PASSIONFRUIT SAUCE

8 passionfruits

¼ cup (2 oz/60 g) sugar

For the mousse, grate the zest (rind) from 2 of the limes, then combine the zest and sugar in a saucepan over low heat. Stir to dissolve the sugar and bring to a boil. Remove from the heat and let stand for 10 minutes.

Reheat the syrup so that it is almost boiling. Dissolve the gelatin in ¼ cup (2 fl oz/60 ml) of cold water set in a saucer of hot water and add to the almost-boiling syrup. Stir to combine.

Place the mangoes in a food processor and process to a purée. Add the grated zest and juice of 1 lime. Stir in the ricotta or mascarpone cheese. Add the gelatin syrup and combine well.

Divide the mousse among twelve 1-cup (8-fl oz/240-ml) molds. Cover with plastic wrap; refrigerate for at least 4 hours.

For the passionfruit sauce, remove the pulp from the passionfruits and place in a bowl. Stir in the sugar and allow to stand for 1 hour to dissolve the sugar. Serve, unmolded, on individual plates with the passionfruit sauce.

Makes 12

Caramelized Peaches with Vanilla Custard

¾ cup (6 oz/180 g) sugar

2 cups (16 fl oz/480 ml) water

4 firm ripe white or yellow peaches

1¼ cups (10 fl oz/300 ml) store-bought or homemade custard

¾ cup (6 fl oz/180 ml), plus 2 tablespoons, light (single) cream

1 teaspoon vanilla extract (essence)

Extra sugar, for broiling (grilling)

Combine the sugar and water in a saucepan and stir over low heat until the sugar dissolves. Bring the mixture to a boil. Add the peaches and poach for 10–15 minutes or until a skewer inserted in the thickest part of the peach meets no resistance.

Remove the peaches, peel off the skins and set aside. Bring the poaching syrup to a boil and boil until reduced by half, about 10 minutes. Set aside to cool slightly.

Combine the custard with the cream, vanilla and 2 tablespoons of the syrup. Place the custard mixture in a bowl and place the peaches in the mixture. Sprinkle the peaches with a little extra sugar. Broil (grill) the peaches, about 2 inches (5 cm) away from the heat, until the sugar caramelizes, about 3 minutes.

Serves 4

Bananas in Cointreau Caramel

¾ cup (6 oz/180 g) firmly packed brown sugar

¾ cup (6 fl oz/180 ml) light (single) cream

⅔ cup (5 oz/150 g) unsalted butter

2 tablespoons Cointreau

4 ripe but firm bananas, sliced

½ cup (2 oz/60 g) pecans, chopped

Plain yogurt (optional), to serve

Combine the brown sugar, cream and butter in a saucepan. Stir over low heat until the sugar dissolves. Bring to a boil, reduce the heat and simmer, stirring, for 3 minutes. Remove from the heat and whisk in the Cointreau. Add the bananas and gently stir until they are coated.

Divide the bananas among four individual serving bowls. Sprinkle with the chopped pecans. Serve with yogurt, if desired.

Serves 4

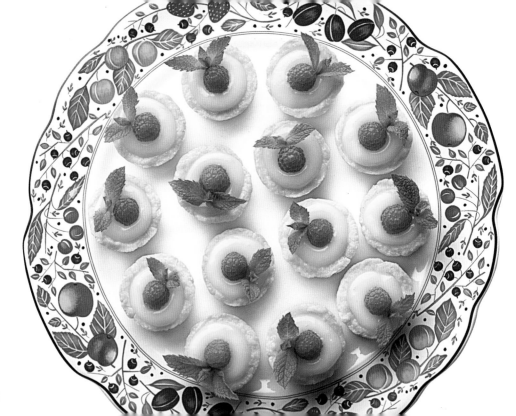

Lemon Curd and Raspberry Tartlets

Tart Pastry (page 17)

LEMON CURD

½ cup (4 oz/120 g) sugar

4 teaspoons cornstarch (cornflour)

1 teaspoon finely grated lemon zest (rind)

¾ cup (6 fl oz/180 ml) water

2 beaten egg yolks

¼ cup (2 fl oz/60 ml) lemon juice

2 tablespoons butter

GARNISH

24 raspberries

24 fresh mint sprigs (optional)

Preheat an oven to 450°F (220°C/Gas Mark 6).

Prepare pastry as directed and shape into twenty-four ¾-inch (2-cm) balls. Press balls into ungreased 1¾-inch (4.5-cm) mini-muffin cups, pressing an even layer onto the bottom and up the sides of each cup.

Bake for 5–8 minutes, or until edges are light brown. Cool the pastry shells in muffin cups on a rack. Remove pastry shells from muffin cups and set aside.

Meanwhile, for the lemon curd, in a small saucepan combine the sugar, cornstarch and lemon zest. Stir in the water. Cook and stir till thickened and bubbly. Gradually stir about half of the hot mixture into the egg yolks; return all to the saucepan. Cook and stir over medium heat until mixture boils. Cook and stir for 2 minutes more. Remove from heat. Stir in the lemon juice and butter, stirring till butter melts.

Spoon about 2 teaspoons of the lemon curd into each pastry shell. Place on a large platter. If desired, cover and chill tartlets for up to 24 hours.

To serve, place a raspberry and, if desired, a sprig of mint on each tartlet.

Makes 24

Chocolate-lined Strawberry Pie

Tart Pastry (page 17)

⅓ cup (2 oz/60 g) semisweet (plain) chocolate, chopped

1 tablespoon butter

¼ cup (2 fl oz/60 ml) whipping cream

1 teaspoon light corn syrup

8 cups (2 lb/960 g) medium strawberries, stems removed

⅔ cup (5 fl oz/150 ml) water

⅔ cup (5 oz/150 g) sugar

2 tablespoons cornstarch (cornflour)

Prepare and bake pastry shell as directed; set aside to cool.

Meanwhile, in the top of a double boiler or in a heatproof bowl set over (not touching) simmering water in a pan, melt chopped chocolate and butter; set aside.

In a heavy saucepan, combine the whipping cream and corn syrup. Bring to a gentle boil. Reduce the heat and cook for 2 minutes. Remove from heat and gradually stir into chocolate mixture. Allow the mixture to cool to room temperature.

Spread the cooled chocolate mixture over the bottom and

up the sides of the baked pastry shell; set aside.

Place 1 cup (4 oz/120 g) strawberries and the water in a food processor. Cover and blend until smooth. Add enough additional water to total 1½ cups (6 fl oz/180 ml) liquid.

In a medium saucepan combine the sugar and cornstarch. Stir in the puréed berry mixture. Cook and stir over medium heat until the mixture is thick and bubbly. Cook and stir, 2 minutes more. Allow to cool for 10 minutes without stirring.

Arrange half of the remaining strawberries, stem end down,

in the pastry shell. Carefully spoon half of the thickened mixture over the berries, thoroughly covering each piece of fruit. Arrange the remaining berries over the first layer. Spoon the remaining thickened mixture over the fruit, covering each piece. Chill for 1–2 hours before serving.

Serves 8

Baked Oatmeal and Apple Dessert

1 lb (480 g) apples, peeled and finely sliced

3 tablespoons, plus ⅓ cup (3 oz/90 g), sugar

¼ cup (2 fl oz/60 ml) water

½ tablespoon lime or lemon zest (rind)

1½ cups (4½ oz/135 g) rolled oats

Pinch of baking soda (bicarbonate of soda)

¼ teaspoon salt

¼ cup (2 oz/60 g) melted butter

Heavy (double) cream (optional), to serve

Preheat an oven to 350°F (180°C/Gas Mark 4). Butter an 8- x 8- x 2-inch (20- x 20- x 5-cm) heatproof dish.

In a frying pan, cook the apples with the 3 tablespoons of sugar and the water over medium heat until the water has evaporated and the apples are just tender. Sprinkle with the lime or lemon zest and set aside.

Mix the oats, the remaining sugar, baking soda and salt in a bowl. Stir in the butter and mix thoroughly to combine.

Spread half the oat mixture over the bottom of the prepared dish and top with the apples. Cover with the remaining oat mixture.

Bake for 35 minutes. Serve hot or cold with cream, if desired.

Serves 8

Key Lime Pie

Pastry for single-crust pie
(page 12)

FILLING

2 egg yolks

1⅓ cups (10½ fl oz/315 ml)
sweetened condensed milk

1½ teaspoons finely shredded
lime zest (rind)

⅓ cup (3 fl oz/90 ml) lime juice

½ cup (4 fl oz/120 ml) water

Few drops of green food coloring
(optional)

MERINGUE

3 egg whites

½ teaspoon vanilla extract
(essence)

¼ teaspoon cream of tartar

⅓ cup (3 oz/90 g) sugar

Prepare and roll out pastry as
directed. Line a 9-inch (23-cm)
pie plate with pastry. Trim and
crimp edge of pastry. Bake pastry
in a preheated 450°F (220°C/
Gas Mark 6) oven for 5 minutes.
Reduce the oven temperature to
325°F (160°C/Gas Mark 3).

Meanwhile, for the filling, in a
bowl beat yolks well with a fork.

Gradually stir in the sweetened
condensed milk and lime zest.
Add lime juice, water and, if
desired, food coloring; mix
well. (The mixture will thicken.)
Spoon into the hot pastry shell.
Bake for 30 minutes. Remove
from the oven.

Increase the oven temperature
to 350°F (180°C/Gas Mark 4).

Meanwhile, for the meringue,
in a bowl combine egg whites,
vanilla extract and cream of
tartar. Beat with an electric
mixer on medium speed, about
1 minute, or until soft peaks
form. Gradually add the sugar,
1 tablespoon at a time, beating

on high speed, for about
4 minutes more, or until
the mixture forms stiff
peaks and the sugar
completely dissolves.

Immediately spread
the meringue over the
hot pie filling, carefully
spreading to the edge
of the pastry to seal and
prevent shrinkage. Bake
for 15 minutes; cool for
1 hour. Chill for 3–6 hours
before serving.

Serves 8

Raspberry Cream Puddings

1 tablespoon (1 envelope) gelatin

1 cup (8 fl oz/240 ml) warm water

3 cups (1½ lb/720 g) fresh or frozen raspberries

½ cup (4 oz/120 g) sugar

2½ cups (20 fl oz/600 ml) heavy (double) cream

Extra raspberries, to garnish

Dissolve the gelatin in the warm water.

Set aside ½ cup (4 oz/120 g) of the raspberries. Combine the remaining raspberries and the sugar in a medium saucepan and cook over low heat until the sugar dissolves. Remove from the heat and let cool for 5 minutes.

Place the raspberry mixture in a food processor or blender and purée until smooth.

Strain through a fine sieve into a bowl and stir in the gelatin.

Divide the reserved ½ cup (4 oz/120 g) raspberries between six

1-cup (8-fl oz/240-ml) pudding molds. Pour 2 tablespoons of the raspberry purée into each mold and then refrigerate for 30 minutes.

Whip the cream until soft peaks form and fold in the remaining raspberry purée. Pour the cream over the set raspberry-gelatin mixture; cover with plastic wrap. Refrigerate for about 30 minutes, or until the cream feels firm.

Remove the plastic wrap and unmold the puddings onto six serving plates. Decorate with the extra raspberries and serve immediately.

Makes 6

Berries with Almond Cookies

ALMOND COOKIES

½ cup (3 oz/90 g), plus
2 tablespoons, blanched almonds

¼ cup (2 oz/60 g) granulated sugar

1 small egg, beaten

1 teaspoon amaretto liqueur

¼ cup (1¾ oz/50 g) superfine (caster) sugar

BERRIES

2 cups (8 oz/240 g) berries such as raspberries, blueberries, blackberries and strawberries

4 tablespoons confectioners' (icing) sugar

1 cup (8 fl oz/240 ml) heavy (double) cream

Preheat an oven to 350°F (180°C/Gas Mark 4). Line a baking sheet with parchment (baking) paper.

For the almond cookies, place the almonds and granulated sugar in a food processor and process to a fine meal. With the machine running, add enough of the beaten egg and amaretto so that the mixture forms a mass. Place the mixture on a work surface and pat together until it forms a cohesive mass.

Place the superfine sugar in a small bowl. Divide the dough into 3 equal parts. Roll each part into a 1-inch (2.5-cm) wide rope. Cut each rope into 6 even pieces, roll each into a ball and then roll each one in the sugar. Place the cookies 1 inch (2.5 cm) apart on the prepared baking sheet. Bake for 15 minutes until pale. Cool on a rack.

For the berries, cut any of the larger berries in half. Pour the cream into a small bowl, add the confectioners' sugar and whip until soft peaks form. Gently fold in the berries and serve with the almond cookies.

NOTE Any leftover cookies can be stored in an airtight container for up to 1 week.

Serves 4

Meringues with Cream and Berries

9 egg whites

2 cups (1 lb/480 g) granulated sugar

Cornstarch (cornflour), for dusting

¾ cup (6 fl oz/180 ml) lemon curd (page 185)

Whipped cream and mixed berries, to serve

Confectioners' (icing) sugar, to serve

Preheat an oven to 300°F (150°C/Gas Mark 2).

For the meringues, beat the egg whites with an electric mixer until soft peaks form. Add the granulated sugar a spoonful at a time, beating well after each addition until stiff peaks form.

Spoon the egg-white mixture into a large pastry (piping) bag fitted with a plain tube (nozzle). Line 2 baking trays with non-stick paper, lightly oil and then dust with cornstarch (cornflour). Pipe the meringue into twenty-four 3–4 inch (7–10 cm) circles, making the edges slightly higher than the middle.

Bake the meringue, 10 minutes, then reduce the oven to 250°F (120°C/Gas Mark 1). Cook for another 25–30 minutes, until the meringues are dry.

Turn the oven off, leaving the meringues to cool in the oven for 10 minutes more with the oven door ajar. Remove from the oven and let cool completely before removing from the paper.

Fill one meringue with lemon curd, top with another and fill with whipped cream and top with berries. Dust with the confectioners' sugar, if desired.

NOTE The unfilled meringues can be stored in an airtight container for 2 weeks.

Serves 6 to 8

Cherry Cake with Almond Streusel

CAKE

¾ cup (6 oz/180 g), plus
1 tablespoon, unsalted butter

1 cup (8 oz/240 g) granulated
sugar

2 eggs

1¾ cups (9 oz/270 g) all-purpose
(plain) flour, sifted

2 teaspoons baking powder

1 cup (8 oz/240 g) bottled
or canned red cherries, pitted
and drained

1 teaspoon ground allspice

STREUSEL TOPPING

¼ cup (2 oz/60 g) unsalted
butter, chopped

⅓ cup (2 oz/60 g) all-purpose
(plain) flour

¼ cup (2 oz/60 g) superfine
(caster) sugar

⅓ cup (1½ oz/45 g) sliced
(flaked) almonds

½ teaspoon ground allspice

Heavy (double) cream or
ice cream (optional), to serve

Preheat an oven to 350°F
(180°C/Gas Mark 4). Butter
an 8-inch (20-cm) springform
pan and line with parchment
(baking) paper or greaseproof
(waxed) paper.

For the cake, cream the butter
and granulated sugar in a bowl
until light and fluffy. Add the
eggs, one at a time, beating well.
Fold in the flour and baking
powder and mix well.

Pour half of the cake batter
evenly into the prepared pan.
Top with the cherries, then
sprinkle with the 1 teaspoon
allspice. Spread the remaining
cake batter over the cherries.

For the streusel topping, rub
the butter into the flour until the
mixture resembles breadcrumbs.
Mix in the superfine sugar and
almonds until well combined.

Press the streusel topping on top of the cake. Sprinkle with the ½ teaspoon allspice.

Bake for 45 minutes, or until a wooden skewer inserted into the middle of the cake comes out clean. Let the cake rest in the pan for 10 minutes before turning out onto a wire rack to cool completely.

Serve warm or cold with the cream or ice cream, if desired.

Serves 10 to 12

Fruit

Orange-glazed Fruit Tartlets

Tart Pastry (page 17)

¼ cup (2 oz/60 g) sugar

2 teaspoons cornstarch
(cornflour)

½ cup (4 fl oz/120 ml)
orange juice

3 cups (12 oz/360 g) fresh fruit,
such as sliced strawberries,
sliced peeled peaches or
nectarines, halved grapes,
raspberries or blueberries

Preheat an oven to 375°F
(190°C/Gas Mark 4).

Prepare the pastry as directed
and divide into 8 portions. On
a lightly floured surface, use
your hands to slightly flatten the
dough. Roll each dough portion
into a 5-inch (13-cm) circle.

Line eight 3- to 3½-inch (7.5-
to 9-cm) fluted tartlet pans with
the pastry. Trim the pastry even
with the edge of each pan. Prick
bottoms and sides of the pastry
with the tines of a fork. Place
the pans on a baking sheet.

Bake for 10–12 minutes, or
until the pastry is light brown.
Cool for several minutes, then
remove from the pans and cool
completely on a rack.

Meanwhile, in a medium
saucepan stir together sugar and
cornstarch. Stir in orange juice.

Cook and stir over medium heat
until thickened and bubbly.
Cook and stir for 2 minutes
more. Gently stir in the fruit.

Divide the fruit mixture evenly
among the baked pastry shells.
If desired, chill before serving.

Makes 8

201

Orange Layer Cake

CAKE

3 eggs

1 cup (8 oz/240 g) granulated sugar

1 teaspoon orange juice

1 teaspoon grated orange zest (rind)

1½ cups (7½ oz/225 g) all-purpose (plain) flour

¼ cup (1½ oz/45 g) cornstarch (cornflour)

1½ teaspoons baking powder

1 teaspoon baking soda (bicarbonate of soda)

1 cup (8 fl oz/240 ml) sour cream

1 cup (8 oz/240 g) unsalted butter, melted

ICING

1 cup (8 oz/240 g) unsalted butter, cut into pieces

2 tablespoons orange juice

3 cups (12 oz/360 g) confectioners' (icing) sugar, sifted

¼ cup (2 fl oz/60 ml) Cointreau or Grand Marnier

Preheat an oven to 350°F (180°C/Gas Mark 4). Butter and flour two 9-inch (23-cm) round cake pans.

For the cake, in a large bowl, combine the eggs with the granulated sugar, orange juice and orange zest and beat until creamy, about 3–4 minutes.

Sift together flour, cornstarch, baking powder and baking soda. In a separate bowl, combine the sour cream and melted butter.

Fold the flour and sour cream mixtures alternately into the egg and sugar mixture.

Pour the mixture evenly into the pans. Bake for 20–25 minutes, or until a skewer inserted into the middle of each cake comes out clean. Cool the cake layers in the pan for 10 minutes before turning out onto a wire rack to cool completely.

For the icing, beat the butter until it is light and fluffy. Stir in the orange juice, and gradually beat in the sugar until smooth.

When each cake is cool, cut it in half horizontally. Place the bottom layer on a serving platter and brush with

the Cointreau or Grand Marnier. Spread with 3–4 tablespoons of icing. Repeat with the remaining layers. To finish, cover the cake with the remaining icing. Cut the cake into wedges and serve.

Serves 10 to 12

Individual Caramel Fruit Puddings

FRUIT PUDDINGS

½ cup (2½ oz/75 g) dried apricots, chopped

⅓ cup (1¾ oz/50 g) pitted prunes, chopped

½ cup (2½ oz/75 g) dried figs, chopped

¼ cup (1¾ oz/50 g) currants

½ cup (4 fl oz/120 ml) dark rum

2 (1¾ lb/840 g) brioche loaves

¾ cup (6 oz/180 g) unsalted butter

½ cup (2½ oz/75 g) firmly packed brown sugar

Whipped cream, to serve

Light (single) cream, to serve

TOFFEE SWIRLS

1 cup (8 oz/240 g) granulated sugar

1 cup (8 fl oz/240 ml) water

CARAMEL SAUCE

1½ cups (12 oz/360 g) brown sugar

½ cup (4 fl oz/120 ml) water

2 cups (16 fl oz/480 ml) heavy (double) cream

For the fruit puddings, combine the dried fruits in a bowl. Pour the rum over and stand, 3 hours.

Preheat an oven to 350°F (180°C/Gas Mark 4). Remove the crusts and then cut the brioche into strips to line the sides of four ¾-cup (6-fl oz/180-ml) pudding molds. Cut circles from the brioche to fit the top and bottom of each mold.

Cream the butter and brown sugar until pale and fluffy. Use this mixture to spread on both sides of the brioche strips and circles. Place 1 circle on the bottom of each mold and cover the sides with the strips. Fill with the fruit and liquid. Top with a brioche circle.

Bake for 15–20 minutes or until the tops are crisp and browned. Run a sharp knife around the edge of each mold to loosen.

INDIVIDUAL CARAMEL FRUIT PUDDINGS

For the toffee swirls, combine the granulated sugar and water in a saucepan and stir over low heat to dissolve the sugar. Bring to a boil and boil until golden, about 5 minutes.

Quickly pour 1 tablespoon of the syrup onto a lightly oiled baking sheet, swirling the spoon to get a spider-web effect. Allow to set hard (about 5 minutes) before carefully removing from the baking sheet.

For the caramel sauce, combine the brown sugar and water in a saucepan. Stir over low heat to dissolve the sugar, bring to a boil and boil until the syrup turns a golden color. Remove from heat and quickly stir in the cream. If the mixture is not smooth, return briefly to low heat and stir until any lumps dissolve.

Cover half of each of 4 serving plates with caramel sauce and the other half with cream. Swirl some of the warm caramel sauce through the cream. Unmold the puddings and place each on a plate. Top with whipped cream and decorate with toffee swirls.

Makes 4

Apple and Poppyseed Cake

⅔ cup (5 oz/150 g) butter

1 cup (8 oz/240 g), plus
1 teaspoon, sugar

3 eggs

2 cups (8 oz/240 g) self-rising
flour, sifted

⅓ cup (2 oz/60 g) all-purpose
(plain) flour, sifted

⅔ cup (5 fl oz/150 ml) milk

½ cup (2¾ oz/80 g) poppyseeds

1 tablespoon finely grated lemon
zest (rind)

2 Granny Smith apples, peeled,
cored and very thinly sliced

Preheat an oven to 350°F
(180°C/Gas Mark 4). Butter a
9-inch (23-cm) round cake pan
and line with parchment (baking)
or waxed (greaseproof) paper.

Beat the butter and 1 cup
(8 oz/240 g) of the sugar in a
bowl until just combined. Add
the eggs, flours, milk, poppyseeds and lemon zest. Continue
to beat on low speed with an
electric mixer until combined.
Then beat on high speed until
the mixture is light and creamy,
about 5 minutes.

Spread the mixture into the
pan. Arrange the apple slices,
overlapping around the top of
the cake, and sprinkle with the
remaining 1 teaspoon of sugar.

Bake for 45 minutes, or until a
wooden skewer inserted in the
middle of the cake comes out
clean. Take the cake out of the
oven and let stand in the pan
for 5 minutes before turning out
onto a rack. Serve warm or cold.

NOTE Cut the apples as thinly
as possible, otherwise the apple
will sink into the middle of the
cake during cooking.

Serves 8 to 10

209

CREAM, CHEESE
AND MILK

English Trifle

SHERRY CUSTARD

3 cups (24 fl oz/720 ml) purchased or homemade custard

3 tablespoons cream sherry

TRIFLE

1 medium-sized vanilla or lemon sponge cake or other plain cake, freshly made and cooled, or purchased

2 cups (16 fl oz/480 ml) heavy (double) cream

¼ cup (1 oz/30 g) confectioners' (icing) sugar

1 cup (4 oz/120 g) raspberries

1 cup (4 oz/120 g) strawberries, hulled and sliced

1 cup (10 oz/300 g) strawberry jam

¾ cup (6 fl oz/180 ml) cream sherry

1 cup (4 oz/120 g) blanched sliced (flaked) almonds, toasted

½ cup (2 oz/60 g) strawberries, hulled and sliced, to garnish

ENGLISH TRIFLE

For the sherry custard, combine the custard and the 3 tablespoons of cream sherry. Whisk until the mixture is thoroughly blended.

For the trifle, cut the cake into slices ¼ inch (5 mm) thick and set aside.

In a bowl, combine the cream and confectioners' sugar. Using an electric mixer on medium to high speed, beat until soft peaks form. Cover and refrigerate.

To assemble the trifle, pour about ½ cup (4 fl oz/120 ml) of the custard mixture into the bottom of a large glass serving bowl. Scatter one-fourth of the raspberries and strawberries over the custard mixture.

Spread one side of the cake slices with the strawberry jam. Arrange enough of the cake slices, jam-side up, in a single layer to cover the custard, then sprinkle about 3 tablespoons of the sherry over the top.

Sprinkle some of the toasted almond slices over the cake. Top with a layer of the whipped cream, spreading the cream to the edge.

Starting with the custard, repeat the layers in the same manner until all the ingredients are used up, ending with a layer of the whipped cream.

Garnish with the ½ cup (2 oz/ 60 g) strawberries. Cover and refrigerate for at least 2 hours before serving.

Serves 6 to 8

Strawberry Cheesecake

CRUST

1½ cups (4½ oz/135 g) graham cracker (sweet wholemeal biscuit) crumbs

2 tablespoons sugar

⅓ cup (3 oz/90 g) unsalted butter, melted

FILLING

3 cups (24 oz/720 g) cream cheese, at room temperature

1¼ cups (10 oz/300 g) sugar

6 eggs, at room temperature

2 cups (16 fl oz/480 ml) sour cream, at room temperature

⅓ cup (2 oz/60 g) all-purpose (plain) flour, sifted

2 teaspoons vanilla extract (essence)

Finely grated zest (rind) and juice of 1 lemon

½ cup (5 oz/150 g) strawberry jam

½ cup (2 oz/60 g) finely chopped, hulled strawberries

12 whole strawberries, hulled

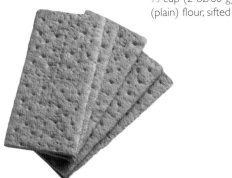

STRAWBERRY CHEESECAKE

Preheat an oven to 350°F (180°C/Gas Mark 4). Butter a springform pan 9½ inches (24 cm) in diameter and 3 inches (7.5 cm) deep.

For the crust, in a medium bowl, combine the crumbs, sugar and melted butter, breaking up any large crumbs and mixing well. Firmly press the mixture evenly over the bottom and 2 inches (5 cm) up the sides of the pan.

For the filling, in a large bowl, break the cream cheese into pieces. Using an electric mixer on medium speed, beat until soft and creamy, 2–3 minutes. Add the sugar and beat until the mixture is smooth, 1–2 minutes. Add the eggs, one at a time, beating well after each addition. Reduce the speed to low and beat in the sour cream, flour, vanilla and lemon zest and juice until thoroughly blended.

Remove 1 cup (8 fl oz/240 ml) of the batter and place it in a small bowl. Add the strawberry jam, mixing thoroughly, and then gently mix in the chopped strawberries. Pour this mixture into the rest of the batter and stir just until incorporated. Pour into the prepared pan and jiggle the pan until the batter is level.

Bake for 1 hour. Turn off the heat and allow the cheesecake to rest undisturbed in the oven until set firm, about 30 minutes longer. Transfer to a rack and allow to cool. Cover and chill overnight before serving.

Just before serving, run a sharp knife around the pan sides to loosen the cake. Release the pan sides and place the cake on a plate. Arrange the whole strawberries evenly around the top, marking a slice with each.

Serves 12

Basque Custard Torte

½ cup (3 oz/90 g) whole blanched almonds or ⅓ cup (1½ oz/45 g) ground almonds

1 cup (8 oz/240 g) sugar

½ cup (4 oz/120 g) unsalted butter, at room temperature

2 egg yolks

1 tablespoon light or dark rum

1½ teaspoons almond extract (essence)

1½ teaspoons Ricard liqueur

Pinch of salt

½ vanilla bean, split lengthwise

1½ cups (7½ oz/225 g) all-purpose (plain) flour

1 teaspoon baking powder

1 cup (8 fl oz/240 ml) pastry cream (page 27), cooled

If using whole almonds, place the nuts in a nut grinder or in a food processor fitted with a metal blade. Grind or process until the nuts are a fine powder. (Do not overprocess.) Set aside.

In a large bowl, using a whisk or an electric mixer on medium speed, beat the sugar and butter until blended. Beat in the egg yolks one at a time, beating well after each addition. Add the rum, almond extract, liqueur and salt. Using the tip of a sharp knife, scrape the seeds from the vanilla bean directly into the bowl. Mix well.

Add the flour, baking powder and ground almonds. Using a wooden spoon or the paddle attachment of the electric mixer on low speed, mix well until the ingredients come together to form a firm dough. Shape into a ball, wrap in plastic wrap and refrigerate for 2–3 hours.

Preheat an oven to 350°F (180°C/Gas Mark 4). Butter and flour a 9-inch (23-cm) round cake pan.

On a lightly floured surface, roll out half of the dough into a round 11 inches (28 cm) in

diameter and ¼ inch (5 mm) thick. Drape the round over the rolling pin and transfer it to the prepared pan. Unwrap the round and press it gently into the pan. Using the rolling pin, roll over the top of the pan to trim away any uneven dough edges. Spread the pastry cream evenly over the bottom of the pastry-lined pan.

Roll out the remaining dough portion into a round about 9 inches (23 cm) in diameter and ¼ inch (5 mm) thick. Place the pan over the dough and,

using the pan edge as a guide, cut out a round the size of the pan. Drape the round over the rolling pin and carefully transfer it to the pan, placing it atop the pastry cream, to form the top layer of the torte.

Bake until the torte is golden brown, 40–45 minutes. Transfer the torte to a rack and let cool for 10 minutes. Invert onto the rack, turn right side up and let cool completely. Transfer to a serving plate and serve at room temperature.

Serves 8

Caramelized Rice Puddings

3 tablespoons dark rum

1 tablespoon water

⅓ cup (2 oz/60 g) raisins

½ cup (3½ oz/105 g) Arborio rice

2½ cups (20 fl oz/600 ml) half-and-half (half cream), or more if needed

½ vanilla bean, split lengthwise

2 egg yolks

½ cup (4 oz/120 g) sugar

¾ cup (6 fl oz/180 ml) heavy (double) cream

6 figs, cut in half through the stem end

In a small saucepan, combine the rum and water and bring to a boil. Remove from the heat, stir in the raisins and let stand until needed.

In the top pan of a double boiler or in a heatproof bowl set over (not touching) simmering water in a pan, combine the Arborio rice, 2½ cups (20 fl oz/600 ml) half-and-half and vanilla bean. Cover and cook until the liquid is absorbed and the rice tender, about 1 hour.

Check the level of the liquid occasionally to make sure the pan does not go dry. If the rice is still a bit tough and all the liquid has been absorbed, add a little more half-and-half and cook until the rice softens. The rice mixture should be very thick.

Remove the top pan, uncover and set aside to cool, 5 minutes. Combine the yolks and ¼ cup (2 oz/60 g) of the sugar in a small bowl and whisk to blend. Whisk in a small amount of the rice mixture to warm the yolk mixture slightly, then whisk the yolk mixture into the rice.

Reposition the top pan over the lower pan of simmering water and cook uncovered, stirring occasionally, until thickened, 3–4 minutes. Remove the top pan and transfer the contents to a bowl. Cover with plastic wrap pressed directly onto the surface of the rice to prevent a skin from forming. Refrigerate until chilled. (The rice can be prepared to this stage up to 1 day beforehand.)

In a bowl, whip the heavy cream until stiff peaks form. Remove and discard the vanilla bean from the rice pudding. Drain the raisins. Using a spatula, fold the cream and the raisins into the rice mixture, distributing the raisins evenly and folding only until no white drifts of cream

remain. Pack the pudding firmly into six ½-cup (4-fl oz/120-ml) flameproof ramekins. Level the surface, cover and refrigerate until well chilled before serving.

To serve, preheat a broiler (griller). Place the ramekins on a baking sheet. Divide the remaining ¼ cup (2 oz/60 g) sugar evenly among the ramekins, sprinkling 2 teaspoons evenly over the surface of each pudding. Place the ramekins in the broiler about 2 inches

(5 cm) from the heat and broil (grill) until the sugar caramelizes, about 3 minutes. Rotate each of the ramekins as needed so they brown evenly. Serve immediately, accompanied by the figs.

Makes 6

Cream Cheese Blintzes with Strawberry Glaze

BLINTZES

1 cup (5 oz/150 g) all-purpose (plain) flour

2 teaspoons superfine (caster) sugar

1 egg, slightly beaten

¾ cup (6 fl oz/180 ml) sour cream

1 cup (8 fl oz/240 ml) milk

¼ cup (2 oz/60 g) unsalted butter

FILLING

¾ cup (4½ oz/135 g) golden raisins (sultanas)

¼ cup (2 fl oz/60 ml) brandy

½ cup (4 oz/120 g) cottage cheese

1 cup (8 oz/240 g) cream cheese, at room temperature

¼ cup (2 oz/60 g) unsalted butter, at room temperature

¼ cup (2 oz/60 g) granulated sugar

2 teaspoons grated lemon zest (rind)

2 tablespoons sour cream

1 egg yolk

Unsalted butter, for cooking

GLAZE

¾ cup (7½ oz/225 g) strawberry jam

2 tablespoons brandy

2 tablespoons water

Raspberries (optional), to serve

For the blintzes, sift the flour and superfine sugar in a bowl, add egg and mix well. Combine the sour cream and milk and gradually add it to the flour mixture; beat with a wooden spoon until the batter is smooth and let stand for 1 hour.

Heat a pancake pan and grease with unsalted butter. Using a small jug, pour ¼ cup (2 fl oz/ 60 ml) of the mixture into the pan, swirling the batter evenly around the pan. Cook the batter over moderate heat until lightly golden. Toss, and cook on the other side for a few minutes. Repeat the process with the remaining batter. (The mixture makes about 10 pancakes.)

For the filling, place the golden raisins in a small saucepan with the brandy and bring to a boil. Reduce the heat and simmer for 2 minutes. Remove from the heat and let stand, 30 minutes. Beat together the cheeses, butter and sugar until creamy. Add the lemon zest, sour cream and egg yolk and mix well.

Drain the sultanas and add them to the cream mixture. Place about ¼ cup (2 fl oz/60 ml) of the cream mixture in the center of a pancake; fold the pancake over the filling to form a parcel. Refrigerate for 2–24 hours before frying. Heat butter in the pancake pan and fry the blintzes until golden brown on both sides.

For the glaze, place the jam, brandy and water in a saucepan and stir until boiling, then pass through a fine sieve.

To serve, arrange the blintzes on a serving plate and spoon on the glaze. If desired, decorate with raspberries.

Serves 8

Profiteroles with Pastry Cream and Toffee Icing

PROFITEROLES

1 cup (8 fl oz/240 ml) water

Pinch of salt

1 tablespoon unsalted butter

1½ teaspoons sugar

1 cup (4 oz/120 g) all-purpose (plain) flour

4 eggs

PASTRY CREAM

3 egg yolks

¼ cup (2 oz/60 g) sugar

2½ tablespoons all-purpose (plain) flour

1 cup (8 fl oz/240 ml) milk

1 teaspoon vanilla extract (essence)

TOFFEE

1 cup (7 oz/210 g) sugar

2 cups (16 fl oz/480 ml) water

Preheat an oven to 375°F (190°C/Gas Mark 4). Lightly grease a large baking sheet.

For the profiteroles, combine the water, salt, butter and sugar in a saucepan. Bring the mixture to a boil. Remove the pan from the heat and stir in the flour, mixing well. Return the saucepan to the heat and cook over medium heat until the dough begins to come away from the sides of the pan. Place the dough in an electric mixer and allow to cool slightly. Add the eggs one at a time, beating well after each addition.

Spoon eight tablespoons of the mixture onto the baking sheet. Bake for 25–30 minutes, until golden brown. Turn off the oven. Make a small incision in each profiterole and return them to the warm oven, leaving the door ajar. Leave for 10–15 minutes, allowing the insides to dry out.

For the pastry cream, put the egg yolks and sugar in a bowl and whisk until pale. Sift in the flour and mix well.

Heat the milk to boiling point and gradually whisk the milk into the yolk mixture. Pour this mixture back into the saucepan and stir over a gentle heat for 7–10 minutes, or until thick. Stir in the vanilla and allow the mixture to cool. Fill each profiterole with pastry cream, using a pastry (piping) bag.

For the toffee, combine the sugar and water in a saucepan and stir over low heat to dissolve the sugar. Bring the mixture to a boil and boil, without stirring, for about 5 minutes, or until golden brown.

Spoon the hot toffee over the filled profiteroles immediately, working quickly, as the toffee will set.

Makes 8

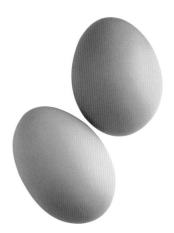

Buttermilk Puddings with Mango Sauce

PUDDINGS

¼ cup (2 fl oz/60 ml), plus 3 tablespoons, heavy (double) cream

½ cup (4 oz/120 g) granulated sugar

1½ teaspoons (½ envelope) gelatin

1 tablespoon water

½ vanilla bean

1 cup (8 fl oz/240 ml) buttermilk

MANGO SAUCE

1 mango, peeled and pitted

1 tablespoon confectioners' (icing) sugar

For the puddings, combine the ¼ cup (2 fl oz/60 ml) cream with the granulated sugar in a saucepan and bring to a boil. Remove from the heat.

Dissolve the gelatin in the water. Stir the gelatin into the cream mixture and mix well. Transfer to a bowl and stir in the buttermilk. Split the vanilla bean and scrape the seeds into the pudding. Refrigerate for 20 minutes, stirring occasionally.

Whip the 3 tablespoons of cream and fold into the cooled mixture. Pour into 2 lightly oiled 1-cup (8-fl oz/240-ml) molds. Fill each mold to the top. Wrap with plastic wrap and refrigerate for 2 hours.

For the mango sauce, place the mango flesh and sugar in a food processor and purée until smooth. Strain through a sieve and reserve the sauce.

Unmold the puddings and serve with the mango sauce.

Makes 2

Greek Cheese Tartlets

PASTRY

2 cups (8 oz/240 g) sifted all-purpose (plain) flour

¼ teaspoon salt

1 teaspoon baking powder

2 tablespoons sugar

3 tablespoons unsalted butter, at room temperature

¼ cup (2 oz/60 g) vegetable shortening

1 egg, slightly beaten

1 tablespoon water, or as needed

FILLING

2 cups (1 lb/480 g) fresh soft cheese such as mizithra, ricotta or farmer or equal parts ricotta and cream cheese

1 cup (8 oz/240 g) sugar

2 tablespoons all-purpose (plain) flour

2 egg yolks

1 teaspoon ground cinnamon

Grated orange or lemon zest (rind) (optional)

Extra cinnamon (optional), to garnish

For the pastry, in a food processor fitted with a metal blade, combine the flour, salt, baking powder and sugar and process briefly to mix. Add the butter and vegetable shortening and process with rapid pulses until the mixture resembles coarse meal. Add the beaten egg and the 1 tablespoon water and process to form a soft dough, adding more water if necessary.

Gather the dough together and place it on a lightly floured work surface. Knead until the dough is smooth and holds together, 5–10 minutes. Wrap in plastic wrap and refrigerate until needed.

GREEK CHEESE TARTLETS

To make the pastry by hand, combine the flour, salt, baking powder and sugar in a bowl and stir to mix. Add the butter and vegetable shortening and, using a pastry blender or 2 knives, cut them into the dry ingredients until the mixture resembles coarse meal. Add the egg and the 1 tablespoon water and, using a fork, stir together until the mixture forms a soft dough, adding more water if necessary.

Gather the dough together, then knead, shape and refrigerate as directed for the food processor method above.

For the filling, in a large bowl, combine the cheese(s), sugar, flour, egg yolks, the 1 teaspoon cinnamon and the orange or lemon zest, if desired. Stir to mix thoroughly.

Preheat an oven to 350°F (180°C/Gas Mark 4).

Divide the dough into 12 equal balls. On a lightly floured work surface, roll out each ball into a round about 4 inches (10 cm) in diameter. Carefully transfer each round to a tartlet tin 2½ inches (6 cm) in diameter, pressing the dough firmly but gently into the tin and fluting the edges. Place the pastry-lined tins on a large baking sheet.

Alternatively, butter a large baking sheet. Form the 4-inch (10-cm) rounds into free-form tart shells, pinching the edges to make a fluted rim, and place on the prepared baking sheet.

Carefully spoon the cheese filling into the tartlet tins or tart shells, gently smoothing the tops with a rubber spatula. Bake until the tops are a pale golden brown, 20–25 minutes.

Transfer to wire racks and allow to cool. Sprinkle with cinnamon, if desired, and serve at room temperature.

Makes 12

Date Ice Cream with Almond Crunch Topping

TOPPING

½ cup (1½ oz/45 g) rolled oats

½ cup (2½ oz/75 g) hulled pumpkin seeds

½ cup (2½ oz/75 g) chopped almonds

1½ tablespoons vegetable oil

1½ tablespoons honey

1½ tablespoons apple juice

⅛ teaspoon salt

DATE ICE CREAM

2 cups (16 fl oz/480 ml) nonfat milk

1 lb (480 g) fresh dates

6 egg yolks

¾ cup (6 oz/180 g) firmly packed brown sugar

3 cups (24 fl oz/720 ml) half-and-half (half cream)

2 teaspoons vanilla extract (essence)

Preheat an oven to 300°F (150°C/Gas Mark 2). Lightly oil a baking sheet or line it with parchment (baking) paper.

For the almond crunch topping, combine the oats, pumpkin seeds and almonds in a medium bowl and stir to mix. In a small saucepan over low heat, combine the vegetable oil, honey, apple juice and salt and stir until the mixture is warm and the salt has dissolved. Pour the warm honey mixture over the oat mixture and toss to coat evenly. Spread out the mixture on the prepared

baking sheet and bake, stirring occasionally, until golden, about 20 minutes. Transfer to a rack and allow to cool, then pack in a small airtight container and place in a freezer until needed.

For the date ice cream, pour the milk into a saucepan and place over low heat. Heat, stirring often with a wooden spoon, until only 1 cup (8 fl oz/240 ml) remains, 18–20 minutes. Remove from the heat and allow to cool completely.

Remove the pits from the dates and chop into pea-sized pieces. Place half of the pieces on a plate and transfer to the freezer

until needed. Place the remainder of the date pieces in a blender, add the cooled milk and purée until smooth.

In a bowl, combine the egg yolks and brown sugar and whisk vigorously until lemon colored. In a saucepan, bring the half-and-half to a rolling boil and immediately pour over the yolk mixture while whisking constantly. Add the date-milk mixture and the vanilla, mix well and set aside to cool completely.

Transfer to an ice-cream maker and freeze according to the manufacturer's instructions. Stir the reserved date pieces

into the ice cream and pack into a freezer container. Place in the freezer until set, 2–4 hours.

To serve, scoop into chilled ice-cream dishes, top with the almond crunch topping and serve at once.

Serves 6

237

Crème Brûlée Tart

Tart Pastry (page 17)

FILLING

3 eggs

⅓ cup (3 oz/90 g) granulated sugar

1 teaspoon vanilla extract (essence)

1¼ cups (10 fl oz/300 ml) light (single) cream or milk

TOPPING

¼ cup (2 oz/60 g) firmly packed brown sugar

2 tablespoons finely chopped pecans

Preheat an oven to 375°F (190°C/Gas Mark 4).

Prepare the pastry as directed. On a lightly floured surface, use your hands to slightly flatten the dough. Roll the dough into an 11-inch (28-cm) circle. Ease the pastry into a 9-inch (23-cm) tart pan; trim the pastry even with the edge of the pan. Line the unpricked pastry shell with a double thickness of foil. Bake for 10 minutes. Remove the foil and bake for 10 minutes more, or until light golden brown.

Meanwhile, for the filling, in a large bowl use a rotary beater or wire whisk to slightly beat the eggs just until mixed. Stir in the granulated sugar and vanilla. Gradually stir in the cream or milk. With the pastry shell on the oven rack, pour the filling into the pastry shell. Reduce the oven temperature to 350°F (180°C/Gas Mark 4).

Bake for 25–35 minutes, or until a wooden skewer inserted into the center comes out clean. Allow to cool completely on a rack, then cover and chill for at least 2 hours before serving.

For the topping, just before serving, press the brown sugar through a sieve evenly over the filling. Sprinkle with the pecans.

Broil the tart 4 inches (10 cm) from the heat for 2–3 minutes, or until the brown sugar begins to melt. Carefully remove the sides of the tart pan and serve immediately.

NOTE The tart may be made a day ahead of when required and topped with the brown sugar and nuts just before serving.

Serves 8 to 12

Baked Cheesecake

CRUST

8 oz (240 g) graham crackers (sweet wholemeal biscuits)

¾ cup (6 oz/180 g) unsalted butter, melted

FILLING

1½ cups (12 oz/360 g), plus 2 tablespoons, ricotta cheese

1 cup (8 oz/240 g) sugar

3 eggs

2 tablespoons all-purpose (plain) flour

1½ cups (12 fl oz/360 ml) sour cream

1 tablespoon lemon juice

1 tablespoon lemon zest (rind)

Preheat an oven to 300°F (150°C/Gas Mark 2).

For the crust, grind the graham crackers in a food processor to fine crumbs. Place the cracker crumbs in a bowl, pour the melted butter over the crumbs and stir to combine. Press into an 8-inch (20-cm) springform pan, lining the base and sides.

For the filling, place the cream cheese, ricotta cheese and sugar in a food processor or electric mixer and process until smooth.

Add the eggs, one at a time, mixing well after each addition. Transfer to a bowl (if using a processor) and fold in the flour, sour cream, lemon juice and lemon zest. Pour the filling into the crust-lined pan.

Bake for 1 hour, or until the cheesecake is set in the middle. Turn off the oven and leave the cheesecake in the warm oven for 15 minutes, with the door ajar. Remove from the oven and cool completely. Refrigerate for at least 2 hours before serving.

Serves 8 to 10

Peanut Butter Cream Pie with Chocolate Lace

CRUST

⅓ cup (3 oz/90 g) butter, melted

1⅓ cups (4 oz/120 g) finely crushed plain chocolate cookies

FILLING

¾ cup (6 fl oz/180 ml) whipping cream

2 tablespoons confectioners' (icing) sugar, sifted

1 teaspoon vanilla extract (essence)

1 cup (8 oz/240 g) cream cheese, softened

½ cup (4 oz/120 g) peanut butter

½ cup (2 oz/60 g) confectioners' (icing) sugar, sifted

¼ cup (2 fl oz/60 ml) milk

CHOCOLATE LACE

½ cup (2½ oz/75 g) semisweet (plain) chocolate, chopped

1½ teaspoons vegetable shortening or butter

For the crust, combine the butter and the crushed cookies. Spread the mixture evenly into a 9-inch (23-cm) pie plate. Press onto the bottom and sides to form a firm, even crust. Chill in refrigerator while preparing the filling.

For the filling, in a medium bowl, beat the whipping cream, the 2 tablespoons confectioners' sugar and the vanilla until soft peaks form; set aside. In a large bowl beat the cream cheese and the peanut butter until light and fluffy. Add the ½ cup (2 oz/60 g) confectioners' sugar and milk; beat until smooth and creamy. Fold the whipped cream mixture into the peanut butter mixture and spoon evenly into the crust. Cover and chill for 4–6 hours.

For the chocolate lace, place the chopped chocolate and vegetable shortening or butter in a heavy

plastic bag. Close the bag and put the section with chocolate into a small bowl of warm water. Let stand until melted. Snip off one corner of the bag. Pipe small designs onto a baking sheet lined with waxed (greaseproof) paper. Let stand until dry, then peel the chocolate from the waxed paper and use to garnish each serving. Store in the refrigerator.

Serves 8

Goat Cheese Cake

4 eggs, separated, at room temperature

5½ oz (165 g) fresh soft goat cheese

3 tablespoons sugar

½ cup (4 fl oz/120 ml) crème fraîche

1 cup (4 oz/120 g) mixed fresh berries, such as raspberries and blackberries

Preheat an oven to 375°F (190°C/Gas Mark 4). Butter an 8-inch (20-cm) round cake pan. Line the bottom with a circle of parchment (baking) paper cut to fit precisely; butter and flour the paper and sides of the pan.

Place the egg whites in a bowl. Using an electric mixer on high speed, beat the whites until they form stiff but moist peaks.

In another bowl, combine the goat cheese and sugar and, using a whisk, beat until well blended. Add the egg yolks, one at a time, beating well after each addition until smooth and creamy.

Using a spatula and working in several batches, carefully fold the beaten whites into the egg yolk mixture. (Do not overmix.) Pour the mixture into the cake pan.

Bake until the cake is golden, puffed and firm to the touch, about 25 minutes. Transfer to

a rack to cool in the pan for 10 minutes, then invert onto the rack, lift off the pan and carefully peel off the paper. Transfer the cake to a serving plate, turn right side up and allow to cool completely.

To serve, spread the crème fraîche evenly over the surface of the cake and then top with the berries. Alternatively, cut into wedges and serve warm, topping each piece with a swirl of crème fraîche and some berries just before serving.

Serves 4 to 6

Sour Cream and Raisin Pie with Meringue

Pastry for single-crust pie (page 12)

1 teaspoon ground cinnamon

FILLING

1 cup (6 oz/180 g) raisins

3 egg yolks

1½ cups (12 fl oz/360 ml) sour cream

1 cup (8 oz/240 g) sugar

½ cup (4 fl oz/120 ml) milk

3 tablespoons all-purpose (plain) flour

1 teaspoon ground cinnamon

¼ teaspoon ground nutmeg

¼ teaspoon ground cloves

MERINGUE

3 egg whites

½ teaspoon vanilla extract (essence)

¼ teaspoon cream of tartar

⅓ cup (3 oz/90 g) sugar

Prepare the pastry as directed, except stir in the 1 teaspoon cinnamon with the flour and salt. Roll out and line a 9-inch (23-cm) pie plate with pastry. Trim and crimp edge of pastry.

For the filling, in a saucepan, add enough water to the raisins to cover. Bring to boiling point and remove from the heat. Cover pan and let stand for 5 minutes. Drain the raisins and set aside.

Preheat an oven to 375°F (190°C/Gas Mark 4).

In a medium bowl, beat the egg yolks just until mixed. Stir in the sour cream, sugar, milk, flour, the 1 teaspoon cinnamon, nutmeg, cloves and raisins.

Pour the mixture into the pastry shell. To prevent overbrowning, cover the edge of the pie with

aluminum foil. Bake the pie for 20 minutes. Remove the foil and bake 20–25 minutes more, or until the center appears nearly set when shaken. Remove pie and reduce oven temperature to 350°F (180°C/Gas Mark 4).

For the meringue, in a bowl, combine the egg whites, vanilla and cream of tartar. Beat with an electric mixer on medium speed until soft peaks form. Gradually add the sugar, 1 tablespoon at a time, beating until stiff peaks form. Spread the meringue over the filling, carefully spreading to the edge of the pastry to seal and prevent shrinkage.

Bake for 15 minutes. Cool on a rack for 1 hour. Chill 3–6 hours before serving.

Serves 8

Crème Brûlée

4 cups (32 fl oz/960 ml) heavy (double) cream

1 vanilla bean, split lengthwise

7 egg yolks

⅔ cup (5 oz/150 g), plus 7 teaspoons, sugar

Preheat an oven to 350°F (180°C/Gas Mark 4).

In a large saucepan, over high heat, combine the cream and vanilla bean and bring to a boil, stirring occasionally with a wire whisk to prevent sticking.

Meanwhile, in a bowl, using the whisk, stir together the egg yolks and the ⅔ cup (5 oz/150 g) sugar until well blended. As soon as the cream boils, remove it from the heat and pour it into the egg-sugar mixture in a steady stream, whisking constantly.

Strain the cream-egg mixture through a fine-mesh sieve into 7 ramekins, 3½ inches (9 cm) in diameter and 2½ inches (6 cm) tall, dividing it evenly.

Place the ramekins in a shallow baking pan and pour in hot water to reach halfway up the sides of the ramekins. Bake until the custard is firm to the touch, about 1 hour and 10 minutes. Remove the baking pan from the oven and the ramekins from the baking pan. Let cool completely, then cover and refrigerate until well chilled, 2–3 hours.

Preheat a broiler (griller).

Sprinkle 1 teaspoon of the sugar evenly over the top of each well-chilled ramekin. Place them on a baking sheet and place the sheet in the broiler about 4 inches (10 cm) from the heat source and broil (grill) until the sugar caramelizes, about 5 minutes.

Remove from the broiler and serve immediately.

Makes 7

Rum and Raisin Rice Pudding

1 cup (7 oz/210 g) short-grain white rice

4 cups (32 fl oz/960 ml) nonfat milk

4 cinnamon sticks

1¾ cups (14 fl oz/420 ml) sweetened condensed milk

1 vanilla bean, split lengthwise

Ice water, as needed

¾ cup (6 fl oz/180 ml) dark rum

1 cup (6 oz/180 g) golden raisins (sultanas)

Ground cinnamon (optional), for dusting

Rinse the rice in several changes of water until the water runs clear. Drain well.

In a saucepan, combine the nonfat milk and the cinnamon sticks and bring to a boil over medium-high heat. Add the rice and return to a boil. Reduce the heat to medium-low and cook uncovered, stirring occasionally, until the centers of the grains are just soft, 12–15 minutes.

Add the sweetened condensed milk to the rice mixture and then scrape the seeds from the vanilla bean halves into the pan. Add the vanilla pods as well, stir to combine, cover and continue to simmer over low heat until the rice is plump and tender and the sauce is the consistency of heavy (double) cream, about 10 minutes longer. Remove from the heat and place over a bowl of ice water to stop the cooking.

Stir the mixture occasionally as it cools. When cool, discard the vanilla pods and the cinnamon sticks and transfer to a bowl. Cover and refrigerate until well chilled, about 2 hours.

Meanwhile, combine the rum and raisins in a heavy-bottomed saucepan over low heat. Simmer until the raisins have plumped and the rum is almost gone, about 5 minutes. Remove from the heat and let cool.

Fold the raisins into the chilled rice pudding. Serve icy cold with a dusting of the ground cinnamon on top, if desired.

Serves 4 to 6

Mexican Custard Squares

3 cups (24 fl oz/720 ml) milk

4 eggs, beaten

½ cup (4 oz/120 g) sugar

1 piece cinnamon stick,
2 inches (5 cm) long

1 strip orange peel, 4 inches
(10 cm) long

¾ cup (4 oz/120 g) cornstarch
(cornflour)

1 egg, beaten

Flour, for coating

⅓ cup (2½ fl oz/75 ml)
vegetable oil

Sugar and ground cinnamon,
for dusting

Whisk together the milk, the 4 beaten eggs, the sugar and the cornstarch in a saucepan. Add the cinnamon stick and orange peel and cook over low heat. Stir with a wooden spatula for 25 minutes until thick. Remove from the heat and discard the orange peel and cinnamon.

Butter an 8- x 12-inch (20- x 30-cm) oblong mold and fill with the milk mixture. Cool, cover with plastic wrap and refrigerate for 8 hours.

Cut the cooled and set mixture into 2- x 2-inch (5- x 5-cm) squares. Dip each square into

the 1 beaten egg and then into the flour. Heat the vegetable oil in a small frying pan and fry the squares for 2–3 minutes on each side until golden brown.

Place on a serving dish and dust with the sugar and cinnamon. Serve warm.

Makes 24

253

Florentine Cheesecake

CRUST

1½ cups (6 oz/180 g) graham cracker (sweet wholemeal biscuit) or shortbread crumbs

1 tablespoon brown sugar

1 tablespoon ground cinnamon

¼ cup (2 oz/60 g) unsalted butter, melted and cooled

FILLING

2 cups (1 lb/480 g) cream cheese

1 cup (8 oz/240 g) ricotta cheese

4 eggs

½ cup (1½ oz/45 g) unsweetened cocoa powder

1 teaspoon vanilla extract (essence)

1 cup (8 oz/240 g) granulated sugar

3 tablespoons brewed strong black coffee

2 teaspoons ground cinnamon

TOPPING

1 cup (8 fl oz/240 ml) sour cream

½ cup (4 oz/120 g) superfine (caster) sugar

1 tablespoon unsweetened cocoa powder

1 teaspoon ground cinnamon

Preheat an oven to 325°F (160°C/Gas Mark 3).

Line a 9-inch (23-cm) spring-form pan with aluminum foil and lightly butter the sides.

For the crust, combine the cracker or shortbread crumbs, brown sugar and cinnamon in a bowl, then stir in the melted butter. Press the mixture into the base of the prepared pan.

For the filling, place the cheeses, eggs, cocoa and vanilla in a food processor and process until smooth. Add the sugar, coffee and cinnamon and continue to beat for 10 minutes, or until the mixture is combined.

Pour into the crust-lined pan and bake for 1 hour, or until firm to the touch. Remove the cake from the oven and allow to stand for 5 minutes before spreading on the topping.

For the topping, combine the sour cream, sugar, cocoa and cinnamon in a bowl and stir thoroughly. Spread over the cooked cheesecake and return to the oven for 10–15 minutes, or until set. Let the cheesecake cool completely in the pan before refrigerating overnight.

To serve, run a knife around the edge of the pan and gently remove the sides.

Serves 10 to 12

NUTS AND COCONUT

Hazelnut and Roasted Almond Mousse Cake

1 génoise (page 26)

MERINGUE

1 cup (8 oz/240 g) sugar

⅓ cup (2½ fl oz/75 ml) water

4 egg whites

HAZELNUT MOUSSE

1 cup (8 oz/240 g) unsalted butter

4 oz (120 g) hazelnut paste

4 egg yolks

1 cup (8 oz/240 g) sugar

2 cups (9 oz/270 g) sugar-roasted almonds (double recipe; page 29)

Prepare and bake the génoise as directed. Allow to cool, cut to form 3 even layers and set aside.

For the meringue, in a small saucepan, bring the sugar and water to a boil. Meanwhile, in a bowl, using an electric mixer on high speed, beat the egg whites until soft peaks form. Continue to boil the sugar-water mixture until it reaches the soft-ball stage, 240°F (115°C) on a candy thermometer.

With the electric mixer set on medium speed, beat the sugar mixture into the egg whites.

Reduce the speed to low and continue beating until stiff peaks form, about 5 minutes. Scoop the meringue onto a baking sheet, spread it out in an even layer and refrigerate until cool.

For the hazelnut mousse, place the butter in a large heatproof bowl. Place over (not touching) gently simmering water in a pan. Let stand until very soft. Add the hazelnut paste and, using a wire whisk, beat until no lumps remain. Remove from the pan and beat in the egg yolks, one at a time, until creamy. Then gently fold in the meringue.

Set aside a 10-inch (25-cm) springform cake pan. Spoon one-third of the mousse into the pan and top with a génoise layer. Repeat the mousse and génoise layers, ending with a génoise layer. Cover and refrigerate until set, about 2 hours.

To unmold, slide a hot knife between the cake and the pan sides. Invert a plate over the pan. Holding the pan and plate together, flip them and lift off the pan. Sprinkle the almonds over and serve immediately.

Serves 8 to 10

Pecan and Chocolate Chip Pie

Pastry for single-crust pie
(page 12)

3 eggs

1 cup (8 fl oz/240 ml) light
corn syrup

1/3 cup (3 oz/90 g) butter, melted

1/2 cup (4 oz/120 g) sugar

1 cup (5 oz/150 g) semisweet
(plain) chocolate, chopped, or
semisweet (plain) chocolate chips

1 cup (4 oz/120 g) pecan halves,
plus 10 pecan halves

1 cup (8 fl oz/240 ml) whipping
cream, whipped

Prepare and roll out pastry as directed. Line a 9-inch (23-cm) pie plate with pastry. Trim and crimp edge of pastry.

Preheat an oven to 350°F (180°C/Gas Mark 4) and line a baking sheet with waxed (greaseproof) paper.

In a medium bowl, use a whisk to slightly beat the eggs. Stir in the corn syrup, melted butter and sugar and mix well. Reserve 2 tablespoons of the chocolate and stir the remaining chocolate and the 1 cup (4 oz/120 g) pecan halves into the filling.

Pour the filling into the pastry shell. To prevent overbrowning, cover the edge of the pie with aluminum foil. Bake for about 25 minutes. Remove the foil and bake for 20–25 minutes more, or until the center appears nearly set when shaken. Cool on a rack.

Meanwhile, in a heatproof bowl set over (not touching) simmering water in a pan, melt the reserved chocolate. Dip one end of each of the 10 pecan halves into the melted chocolate. Place on the baking sheet and refrigerate until the chocolate is firm, 15 minutes.

Serve with whipped cream and the chocolate-dipped pecans. Store in the refrigerator.

Serves 10

Cream Puffs Praline

Cream Puff Pastry (page 24)

GLAZED PECANS

¾ cup (3 oz/90 g) pecan halves

¼ cup (2 oz/60 g) granulated sugar

1 tablespoon butter

¼ teaspoon vanilla extract (essence)

10 scoops vanilla ice cream

PECAN SAUCE

¾ cup (6 oz/180 g) granulated sugar

¾ cup (6 oz/180 g) firmly packed brown sugar

½ cup (4 fl oz/120 ml) half-and-half or light (single) cream

3 tablespoons butter

½ cup (2 oz/60 g) chopped toasted pecans

Preheat an oven to 400°F (200°C/Gas Mark 5) and lightly grease a baking sheet.

Prepare the pastry as directed. Form the cream puffs by heaping tablespoonfuls into 10 mounds, 3 inches (7.5 cm) apart, onto the prepared baking sheet. Bake for 30 minutes, or until golden brown. Remove the puffs from the pan and cool on a wire rack.

Meanwhile, for the glazed pecans, line a baking pan with aluminum foil and lightly grease. In a heavy skillet, combine the pecan halves, ¼ cup (2 oz/60 g) granulated sugar, the butter and vanilla. Cook over medium-high heat, shaking the skillet, until the sugar begins to melt. (Do not stir.) Reduce the heat to low. Cook until the sugar is melted and golden brown, now stirring frequently.

Remove from the heat and pour into the prepared pan. Cool completely and break into small pieces. Place the ice cream in a chilled bowl. Use a wooden spoon to stir the ice cream to soften it slightly and stir in the glazed pecans. Cover and freeze.

For the pecan sauce, in a heavy saucepan, combine the ¾ cup (6 oz/180 g) granulated sugar, the brown sugar, half-and-half or light cream and butter. Cook over medium-high heat until boiling, stirring constantly. Reduce the heat. Cook and stir for 5 minutes more, or until slightly thickened. Stir in the pecans and keep warm.

To assemble, cut off the top fourth of each cream puff. Remove any soft dough from inside. Place one scoop of the ice-cream mixture into each cream puff. Replace the tops and drizzle each cream puff with warm pecan sauce. Serve immediately.

Makes 10

Baklava

4 cups (1 lb/480 g) almonds, walnuts or equal parts almonds and walnuts, coarsely chopped

¾ cup (6 oz/180 g) sugar

1 tablespoon ground cinnamon

¼ teaspoon ground cloves

1 cup (8 oz/240 g) clarified unsalted butter, melted

1 lb (480 g) filo dough, thawed in the refrigerator if frozen

LEMON SYRUP

2 cups (16 fl oz/480 ml) water

2 cups (1 lb/480 g) sugar

2 lemon zest (rind) strips, each 3 inches (7.5 cm) long

2 tablespoons fresh lemon juice

BAKLAVA

Preheat an oven to 350°F (180°C/Gas Mark 4).

In a bowl, combine the nuts, sugar, cinnamon and cloves.

Brush a 9- x 14- x 2-inch (23- x 35- x 5-cm) baking pan with some of the melted butter. Remove the filo sheets from their package, lay them flat on a work surface and cover with a damp towel or plastic wrap to prevent them from drying out. Lay a filo sheet in the prepared pan and brush it lightly with the butter. Working with 1 sheet at a time, top with half of the remaining filo sheets (about 10 sheets), brushing each sheet with butter after it is placed in the pan.

Spread the nut mixture evenly over the stack of filo sheets. Top with the remaining filo sheets, again brushing each sheet lightly with butter, including the top sheet. Cover and refrigerate for about 30 minutes so the butter will set. (This step makes the baklava easier to cut.)

Using a sharp knife, cut the baklava all the way through into diamond shapes, forming about 36 pieces in all. Bake until golden brown, 35–40 minutes.

Meanwhile, for the lemon syrup, in a saucepan, combine the water, sugar and lemon zest. Bring to a boil, reduce the heat to low and simmer until the

mixture thickens, 12–15 minutes. Remove the lemon zest and discard. Stir in the lemon juice.

Remove the baklava from the oven. Pour the hot syrup evenly over the hot pastry. Let stand for 30 minutes to cool slightly, then recut the diamonds. Serve warm or at room temperature. Store the leftover pieces, covered, at room temperature.

Makes 36

Hazelnut Tart

PASTRY

1 cup (5 oz/150 g) hazelnuts

1 cup (5 oz/150 g) unbleached all-purpose (plain) flour

¼ cup (2 oz/60 g) sugar

⅓ cup (3 oz/90 g) unsalted butter, melted

FILLING

⅓ cup (3 oz/90 g) cream cheese, at room temperature

½ cup (4 oz/120 g) ricotta cheese

⅓ cup (3 oz/90 g) sugar

1½ tablespoons unsweetened cocoa powder

2 egg yolks, plus 1 whole egg

1½ tablespoons Frangelico liqueur

½ cup (2½ oz/75 g) coarsely chopped bittersweet (plain) chocolate

Preheat an oven to 325°F (160°C/Gas Mark 3).

For the pastry, spread the nuts in a single layer on a baking sheet and place in the oven until they just begin to change color and the skins begin to loosen, 8–10 minutes.

Spread the warm hazelnuts on a kitchen towel. Cover with another kitchen towel and rub against the nuts to remove as much of the skins as possible. Let cool, then set aside ¾ cup (3½ oz/105 g) of the nuts to use for the filling. Finely chop the remaining nuts and place in a small bowl.

Increase the oven temperature to 350°F (180°C/Gas Mark 4).

Add the flour and sugar to the chopped hazelnuts and stir to mix. Pour in the melted butter and stir to distribute evenly. The pastry dough should be moist but still crumbly. Transfer the dough into a 9-inch (23-cm) tart pan with a removable bottom. Using your fingertips, press it evenly over the bottom and sides of the pan. Chill for 15 minutes.

Remove the pastry-lined pan from the refrigerator and line with a sheet of aluminum foil or parchment (baking) paper. Fill with pie weights or dried beans. Bake the pastry until the bottom

is just set, about 15 minutes. Remove the pastry from the oven and remove the weights or beans and the foil or paper. Return the pastry to the oven and continue to bake until the pastry is lightly golden and pulls away from the sides of the pan, about 5 minutes longer. Transfer to a rack to cool completely.

Meanwhile, for the filling, in a food processor fitted with a metal blade, combine the cream cheese, ricotta cheese, sugar and unsweetened cocoa. Process until very smooth, stopping to scrape down the sides of the bowl as needed. Add the egg yolks and whole egg and again

process until smooth. Add the Frangelico liqueur and combine.

Pour the filling into the tart shell and jiggle the pan to level the filling. Coarsely chop the reserved hazelnuts and scatter them evenly over the surface along with the chocolate.

Bake until the center is just set, 25–30 minutes. Transfer to a rack and let cool before serving.

Serves 8 to 10

Chocolate Almond Tart

Tart Pastry (page 17)

3 eggs

¾ cup (6 oz/180 g) firmly packed brown sugar

½ cup (4 fl oz/120 ml) dark corn syrup

2 tablespoons dark molasses

⅓ cup (3 oz/90 g) unsalted butter, melted

2 teaspoons vanilla extract (essence)

2 teaspoons ground cinnamon

1 teaspoon salt

2 cups (9 oz/270 g) slivered blanched almonds

¾ cup (4 oz/120 g) chopped semisweet (plain) chocolate

Prepare the pastry as directed. On a lightly floured surface, roll out the ball of dough into a round about 12 inches (30 cm) in diameter and ⅛–¼ inch (3–5 mm) thick. Transfer to a 10-inch (25-cm) tart pan with a removable bottom. Ease the pastry into the tart pan, pressing it gently against the bottom and sides. Trim the edges even with the rim. Chill for 15 minutes.

Preheat an oven to 325°F (160°C/Gas Mark 3).

Prick the bottom and sides of the pastry with a fork. Bake until golden, 10–12 minutes. Transfer to a rack to cool. Leave the oven set at 325°F (160°C/Gas Mark 3).

In a large bowl, whisk together the eggs, brown sugar, corn syrup, molasses, melted butter, vanilla and cinnamon until well blended. Add the salt, almonds and chocolate and mix to coat.

Pour the filling into the tart shell and bake until the center is set, 35–40 minutes. To test, press gently on top with your fingertips. Transfer to a rack and let cool.

To serve, remove the pan sides and, using a spatula, slide off the pan bottom onto a serving plate. Cut into wedges and serve.

Serves 6 to 8

Rich Almond Cake

CAKE

9 eggs, separated

¼ cup (2 fl oz/60 ml) brandy, amaretto or rum

1 teaspoon vanilla extract (essence)

1 cup (8 oz/240 g) sugar

2¼ cups (9 oz/270 g) ground almonds

¾ cup (3 oz/90 g) dried bread crumbs

2 teaspoons baking powder

½ cup (4 oz/120 g) sugar

SYRUP

2 tablespoons brandy, amaretto or rum

1 tablespoon sugar

FILLING AND TOPPING

1¼ cups (10 fl oz/300 ml) heavy (double) cream, whipped

1¼ cups (5 oz/150 g) sliced (flaked) almonds, toasted

Preheat an oven to 300°F (150°C/Gas Mark 2). Butter two 8-inch (20-cm) round cake pans and line with parchment (baking) or waxed (greaseproof) paper.

For the cake, combine the egg yolks, brandy, amaretto or rum,

vanilla and sugar in a large bowl and beat until pale and thick, 3–4 minutes. Stir in the ground almonds, bread crumbs and baking powder. In a separate bowl, beat the egg whites until stiff. Gradually add the sugar and beat until dissolved, about 1 minute. Fold one-third of the egg whites into the egg yolk mixture, then fold in the remaining egg whites.

Pour the mixture into the pans. Bake for 45 minutes, or until a wooden skewer inserted into the center of the cake comes out clean. Cool for 2–3 minutes before turning out onto a wire rack to cool completely.

For the syrup, combine the brandy, amaretto or rum and sugar in a small saucepan and stir over low heat to dissolve the sugar. Make holes in the top of each cake layer using a wooden skewer and brush with syrup.

For the filling and topping, place the bottom cake layer on a serving plate and spread the sides and top with half of the cream. Set the other cake layer on top and cover with the remaining cream. Press the toasted almonds onto the cake and serve immediately.

Serves 8 to 10

Pistachio and Chestnut Cream Mousse Cake

1 génoise layer, ½ inch (12 mm) thick (page 26)

Crème Anglaise (page 28)

4 gelatin leaves

1 oz (30 g) pistachio paste

2 oz (60 g) canned or homemade chestnut purée

1½ cups (12 fl oz/360 ml) heavy (double) cream

½ cup (2 oz/60 g) finely chopped pistachio nuts

2 tablespoons confectioners' (icing) sugar

Prepare and bake the génoise as directed and allow to cool completely before slicing.

Prepare the crème anglaise as directed and allow to cool.

Place 2 gelatin leaves in each of 2 small bowls. Add enough water to cover to both bowls and let stand until softened, about 5 minutes.

Combine ½ cup (4 fl oz/120 ml) of the cooled crème anglaise and the pistachio paste in a blender and mix on high speed until smooth, about 15 seconds.

Transfer to a small saucepan over medium heat and heat until warm. Lift out 2 of the gelatin leaves and add to the warm pistachio mixture. Whisk to mix well and set aside.

Put the remaining half of the crème anglaise and the chestnut purée in a blender and mix on high speed until smooth, about 15 seconds. Transfer to another small saucepan over medium heat and heat until warm. Lift out the remaining 2 gelatin leaves and add to the chestnut mixture. Whisk well to combine.

In a bowl, place ¾ cup (6 fl oz/ 180 ml) of the cream. Using an electric mixer set on high speed, beat until soft peaks form. Add the pistachio mixture and beat on low just until combined, about 30 seconds.

Place the génoise layer in a springform cake pan 10 inches (25 cm) in diameter and 2 inches (5 cm) deep. Pour the pistachio mixture over the génoise layer, and refrigerate until set, about 10 minutes.

In a clean bowl, place the remaining cream. Using the electric mixer set on high speed, beat until soft peaks form. Add

the chestnut mixture and beat on low just until combined, about 30 seconds.

Pour the chestnut mixture over the set pistachio mixture, cover and refrigerate for 4 hours.

To unmold, run hot water over a knife blade, wipe dry, and slide the blade between the cake and the pan sides. Release the pan sides and slide the cake onto a plate. Sprinkle on the pistachio nuts and sift the confectioners' sugar over the top.

Serves 8

About Chestnuts

Equally at home in sweet and savory dishes, the versatile chestnut was once a staple food, used for grinding into a flour long before grains and potatoes took over that role. Chestnuts must be boiled or roasted before they can be eaten and, of course, encouraged to shuck off that troublesome and reluctant shell. Chestnuts with shells on will yield about half of the original weight when shelled. It is possible to buy shelled chestnut meat ready frozen for use, as well as chestnut purée in jars and cans, both of which are a great convenience to the cook.

However chestnuts are to be cooked, their shells must be cut before heating or they will explode. Take a sharp knife and cut an X on the flat side of each nut. To roast chestnuts, spread them in a shallow pan and roast in a 400°F (200°C/Gas Mark 5) oven for 25–30 minutes, or until chestnuts feel tender when pressed and the shells have curled where they were cut. Remove from the oven and, using a small, sharp knife, remove the shells and the furry skin directly underneath. (Chestnuts should be peeled while still warm.) They are now ready to be puréed or treated in any way called for by the recipe.

To boil chestnuts, slash the skins as above and simmer for 15 minutes. Remove only one chestnut at a time and peel off the outer and inner skins. It is impossible to remove the inner skin if the nut has gone cold. Chestnuts can also be spread on a glass plate and microwaved for 5–6 minutes, stirring several times. Stand for 5 minutes and keep warm while peeling.

Coconut Savarin

SAVARIN

1 envelope (¼ oz/7 g) active dry yeast

¼ cup (2 fl oz/60 ml) warm water

¼ cup (5 oz/150 g) sugar

1 cup (4 oz/125 g) all-purpose (plain) flour

⅓ cup (1 oz/30 g) flaked (desiccated) coconut

¼ cup (2 oz/60 g) butter, melted

2 eggs, slightly beaten

SYRUP

1 cup (8 oz/240 g) sugar

1 cup (8 fl oz/240 ml) water

2 cups (12 oz/360 g) sliced fresh peaches, plums, nectarines or apricots

⅓ cup (3½ oz/105 g) apricot jam

½ cup (4 fl oz/125 ml) brandy

Preheat an oven to 400°F (200°C/Gas Mark 5). Lightly butter a 9-inch (23-cm) ring or savarin mold.

For the savarin, dissolve the yeast in the warm water. Stir in a pinch of the sugar, then set aside in a warm place to proof, 5–10 minutes, until creamy.

Combine the flour, coconut and sugar in a bowl. Make a well in the center and add the yeast mixture, butter and eggs. Mix until combined. Cover with a damp cloth and stand in a warm place until dough has doubled in size, 20–30 minutes.

Press the dough into the ring or savarin mold. Bake for 5 minutes, then reduce the heat to 350°F (180°C/Gas Mark 4) and bake for a further 15 minutes, or until the savarin feels firm. Turn out onto a rack and place over a tray. Pierce all over with a skewer.

For the syrup, place the sugar and water in a saucepan. Boil the mixture for 5 minutes, then reduce the heat to a simmer. Using a slotted spoon, blanch the sliced fruit in the syrup for about 1 minute. Lift out the fruit to drain and set aside.

Strain the syrup through a sieve. Add the apricot jam and brandy and reheat. Pour the hot syrup over the savarin. Arrange the poached fruit in the center of the savarin and serve.

Serves 8 to 10

Almond Cake

1 cup (8 oz/240 g), plus
1 tablespoon, sugar

1½ cups (8 oz/240 g) blanched
almonds

4 eggs

½ cup (4 oz/120 g), plus
1 tablespoon, butter, softened

⅓ cup (3 oz/90 g) apricot jam

3 tablespoons sliced (flaked)
almonds, toasted

Preheat an oven to 350°F
(180°C/Gas Mark 4).

Process the 1 cup (8 oz/240 g)
sugar and the almonds in a food
processor until well ground and
paste-like. With the motor still
running, add the eggs one at a
time. Add the ½ cup (4 oz/120 g)
butter, scraping down the bowl
when necessary. Process until
well blended and smooth.

Butter a 9-inch (23-cm) springform cake pan with the 1 tablespoon of butter. Pour the batter
into the pan and sprinkle the
1 tablespoon sugar over the top.

Bake for 35 minutes, or until a
wooden skewer inserted into the
center comes out clean. Allow
the cake to cool on a wire rack
for 10 minutes before unmolding.
Remove the sides of the pan and
transfer the cake carefully, using
2 spatulas, to a serving plate.

To decorate, spread the apricot
jam around the top edges of the
cake and sprinkle with the sliced
almonds so they stick to the jam.
Slice and serve.

Serves 8

Poppyseed and Hazelnut Kugelhopf

¾ cup (6 fl oz/180 ml) milk

1 envelope (¼ oz/7 g) active dry yeast

3 cups (12 oz/360 g) all-purpose (plain) flour

Pinch of salt

¼ cup (2 oz/60 g) granulated sugar

3 eggs, slightly beaten

½ cup (4 oz/120 g) unsalted butter, melted

½ cup (1¾ oz/50 g) poppyseeds

¼ cup (2 fl oz/60 ml) milk

½ cup (2 oz/60 g) ground hazelnuts

Grated zest (rind) of 3 oranges

¼ cup (2 fl oz/60 ml) orange juice

Confectioners' (icing) sugar, for dusting

Preheat an oven to 375°F (190°C/Gas Mark 4). Generously butter an 8-inch (20-cm) fluted kugelhopf mold or bundt pan.

Heat the milk slowly to body temperature (100°F/37°C), then pour onto the yeast and stir until dissolved. Sift the flour and salt into a warmed bowl, making a well in the center. Add the yeast

mixture, granulated sugar, eggs and butter and beat well. Divide the mixture into 3 equal portions.

To the first portion, add the poppyseeds and 2 tablespoons of the milk. Mix well, ensuring that the poppyseeds are evenly distributed through the dough.

To the second portion, add the hazelnuts and the remaining 2 tablespoons of milk, again beating until the ingredients are well mixed.

To the third portion, add the orange zest and orange juice and mix well.

Spoon small amounts of the dough into the mold, alternating the 3 portions, until all of the dough is used. Cover with a damp cloth and let stand in a warm place for 25–30 minutes, or until the dough has doubled in bulk and almost fills the mold.

Bake for 60–80 minutes, or until a wooden skewer inserted in the middle of the cake comes out clean. Stand for 10 minutes in the mold, then turn out onto a rack to cool completely. Dust with confectioners' sugar and serve immediately.

Serves 10 to 12

Pecan and Sour Cream Cake

¾ cup (6 oz/180 g), plus
1 tablespoon, granulated sugar

⅔ cup (5½ oz/165 g) butter,
chopped into small pieces

1 teaspoon vanilla extract
(essence)

2 eggs

1 cup (4 oz/120 g) ground
almonds

1 cup (4 oz/120 g) self-rising
flour

½ teaspoon baking soda
(bicarbonate of soda)

¾ cup (6 fl oz/180 ml), plus
1 tablespoon, sour cream
or crème fraîche

1¼ cups (5 oz/150 g) chopped
pecans

1 teaspoon ground cinnamon

2 tablespoons light brown sugar

Melted butter (optional),
for glazing

Preheat an oven to 350°F
(180°C/Gas Mark 4). Butter a
9-inch (23-cm) springform pan.

In a food processor, combine
the granulated sugar, butter,
vanilla, eggs, ground almonds,
flour, baking soda and sour
cream. Process for 1–2 minutes,
or until the mixture is smooth.

Pour half of the batter into
the prepared pan. Combine the
pecans, cinnamon and brown
sugar and sprinkle half over the
mixture in the pan. Top with the
second half of the cake mixture
and sprinkle with the remaining
pecan, cinnamon and brown
sugar mixture.

Bake for 1 hour, or until a
wooden skewer inserted in the
middle of the cake comes out
clean. Cool in the pan on a rack
for 10–15 minutes. Turn out
onto a rack to cool completely.
Brush the cake with the melted
butter, if desired, and serve.

Serves 8 to 10

Pecan Coffee Cake

CAKE

¾ cup (6 oz/180 g) butter, softened

1½ cups (12 oz/360 g) granulated sugar

3 eggs

2 teaspoons vanilla extract (essence)

2⅓ cups (12 oz/360 g) all-purpose (plain) flour

1½ teaspoons baking powder

1½ teaspoons baking soda (bicarbonate of soda)

½ teaspoon salt

2 cups (16 fl oz/480 ml) sour cream

FILLING

⅔ cup (5 oz/150 g) firmly packed brown sugar

1 tablespoon ground cinnamon

1½ tablespoons unsweetened cocoa powder

¾ cup (4½ oz/135 g) raisins

¾ cup (3 oz/90 g) chopped pecans

ICING

⅔ cup (5 fl oz/150 ml) whipping cream

1 tablespoon strong black coffee

1–2 tablespoons confectioners' (icing) sugar, sifted

Preheat an oven to 350°F (180°C/Gas Mark 4). Butter a 9-inch (23-cm) springform pan. Line the base with parchment (baking) paper.

For the cake, cream the butter and granulated sugar until light and fluffy. Beat in the eggs one at a time, beating well after each. Add the vanilla. Sift together the flour, baking powder, baking soda and salt. Fold in the sifted dry ingredients alternating with the sour cream, beginning and ending with the flour mixture. Spread a third of the batter into the prepared pan.

For the filling, combine the brown sugar, cinnamon, cocoa, raisins and pecans and mix well. Sprinkle half of the pecan filling over the first layer of batter. Continue layering the batter and filling, finishing with a layer of batter. Tap the pan several times to expel any bubbles. Bake the cake for 50–60 minutes, or until a skewer inserted in the middle of the cake comes out clean. Cool in the pan for 10 minutes, then turn onto a rack.

For the icing, whip the cream. Fold in the coffee and then the sugar and mix well. When the cake is cool, spread the icing over the top and serve.

Serves 10 to 12

Pine Nut Cake

2 large eggs

1¾ cups (14 oz/420 g) sweetened condensed milk

1 cup (5 oz/150 g) pine nuts

Confectioners' (icing) sugar, for dusting

Preheat an oven to 350°F (180°C/Gas Mark 4). Butter a round 9-inch (23-cm) cake pan and line the bottom with waxed (greaseproof) paper. Butter the pan again and flour lightly.

Put the eggs, milk and pine nuts in a blender and blend, stopping to scrape the pine nuts off the sides of the blender as needed, until completely smooth.

Pour the mixture into the pan and bake for about 50 minutes, or until a skewer inserted into the center of the cake comes out clean.

Cool the cake on a wire rack for 10 minutes, then unmold the cake, bottom-side up. Sprinkle the top with confectioners' sugar just before serving.

Serves 10

Mixed Nut Tart

PASTRY

1½ cups (7½ oz/225 g) all-purpose (plain) flour

⅔ cup (5 oz/150 g) cold unsalted butter

2 tablespoons granulated sugar

1 whole egg

1–2 tablespoons cold water

1 egg white, beaten

FILLING

6 eggs, beaten

1 cup (7 oz/210 g) firmly packed brown sugar

¾ cup (6 fl oz/180 ml) light corn syrup or golden syrup

⅓ cup (3 oz/90 g) unsalted butter, melted

½ cup (2½ oz/75 g) hazelnuts

½ cup (2½ oz/75 g) macadamia nuts

½ cup (2 oz/60 g) pecan halves

½ cup (2 oz/60 g) walnut halves

Preheat an oven to 350°F (180°C/Gas Mark 4).

For the pastry, place the flour, butter and sugar in a food processor and process to a coarse meal. Add the egg and 1 tablespoon of the water and pulse until the mixture comes together. (It may be necessary to add more water, a little at a time, until the mixture comes together.) Remove the pastry from the food processor and wrap in plastic wrap. Refrigerate for 30 minutes.

Roll out the pastry and line a 9-inch, 2-inch deep (23-cm, 5-cm deep) tart pan. Cover with parchment (baking) or waxed (greaseproof) paper and sprinkle with baking weights, dried beans or rice. Bake for 15 minutes.

For the filling, combine the eggs, brown sugar, syrup and melted butter in a bowl. Mix until combined and then stir in the nuts. Remove the pastry from the oven and remove the weights and paper.

Brush the pastry with beaten egg white and pour the filling into the tart shell. Return to the oven and bake for about 45 minutes, until the filling just wobbles when shaken. Remove from the oven and allow to cool before serving.

Serves 8 to 10

Hazelnut Macaroons

MACAROONS

½ cup (2½ oz/75 g) whole hazelnuts

1½ cups (6 oz/180 g) confectioners' (icing) sugar

¼ teaspoon baking soda (bicarbonate of soda)

2 egg whites

FILLING

1 lb (480 g) mascarpone cheese

¼ cup (2 fl oz/60 ml) chocolate syrup

2 tablespoons instant coffee granules

2 teaspoons confectioners' (icing) sugar, plus extra for dusting

Preheat an oven to 350°F (180°C/Gas Mark 4).

For the macaroons, place the hazelnuts on a baking tray and roast for 10 minutes. Remove from the oven and process to a fine meal. Sift the 1½ cups (6 oz/180 g) confectioners' sugar and baking soda, add the ground hazelnuts and mix well. Beat the egg whites until stiff and fold in the hazelnut mixture.

Reduce the oven temperature to 225°F (110°C/Gas Mark ½). Line a baking sheet with waxed (greaseproof) paper. Using a pastry (piping) bag, pipe twelve 3-inch (7.5-cm) rounds onto the baking sheet.

Bake for 35 minutes and set aside to cool.

For the filling, divide the mascarpone into 2 bowls. Add the chocolate syrup to 1 bowl and stir to combine. Add the coffee and the 2 teaspoons of confectioners' sugar to the other bowl and stir to combine.

Using a pastry bag, pipe a layer of the chocolate mixture onto one-third of the macaroons. Top each with another macaroon and pipe on a layer of the coffee mixture. Top each with a third macaroon and dust with the confectioners' sugar to serve.

Serves 4

Pecan Tartlets

PASTRY

2 cups (10 oz/300 g) all-purpose (plain) flour

2 teaspoons granulated sugar

⅔ cup (5 oz/150 g) cold unsalted butter

1 egg yolk

1–2 tablespoons ice water

FILLING

2 eggs

½ cup (3½ oz/105 g) firmly packed brown sugar

¼ cup (2 fl oz/60 ml) light corn syrup or golden syrup

2½ tablespoons unsalted butter, melted

½ cup (2 oz/60 g) chopped pecans

½ cup (2 oz/60 g) pecan halves

Crème fraîche, to serve

Preheat an oven to 325°F (160°C/Gas Mark 3).

For the pastry, place the flour, granulated sugar and butter in a food processor. Process to coarse crumbs. Add the egg yolk and 1 tablespoon of the ice water and pulse until the dough comes

together—if necessary add a little more water. Roll out the pastry to a thickness of ½ inch (1 cm).

Line two 4-inch (10-cm) tartlet pans that have removable bases with the pastry. (Any leftover pastry can be kept, frozen, for up to 1 month.) Line the pastry shells with parchment (baking) or waxed (greaseproof) paper and fill with baking weights, dried beans or rice. Bake for 10 minutes. Remove from the oven. Remove the weights and paper and set aside.

For the filling, beat the eggs. Stir in the brown sugar and light corn or golden syrup. Stir in the butter and chopped pecans and combine thoroughly. Pour the mixture into the pastry shells. Arrange the pecan halves in a pattern on top.

Bake for 20–25 minutes, or until the pastry is lightly browned and the middle of the tartlets are set. Remove from the oven and allow to cool a little before unmolding and serving with crème fraîche.

Makes 2

Almond Puddings

¾ cup (6 fl oz/180 ml) milk

½ cup (2 oz/60 g) blanched slivered almonds, ground to a coarse meal

1½ teaspoons (½ envelope) gelatin

1 tablespoon water

2 tablespoons sugar

½ teaspoon vanilla extract (essence)

½ cup (4 fl oz/120 ml) heavy (double) cream, whipped

Combine the milk and ground almonds in a saucepan. Place over moderate heat and bring to boiling point. Remove from the heat and set the mixture aside for 10 minutes. Strain through a fine sieve into a bowl.

Meanwhile, dissolve the gelatin in the water. Stir the gelatin into the strained milk along with the sugar. Allow to cool, stirring occasionally. Stir in the vanilla. Cover and refrigerate until the mixture begins to set, about 20 minutes.

Fold in the whipped cream.

Lightly oil two 1-cup (8 fl oz/240 ml) metal molds. Pour in the pudding mixture so that they are completely full.

Cover with plastic wrap and refrigerate for at least 2 hours until set. Remove the plastic wrap, unmold and serve the puddings immediately.

Makes 2

Coconut Custard Pie

Tart Pastry (page 17)

FILLING

¾ cup (6 oz/180 g) granulated sugar

¼ cup (1 oz/30 g) cornstarch (cornflour)

¼ teaspoon salt

4 egg yolks

3 cups (24 fl oz/720 ml) milk

3 tablespoons unsalted butter

1½ teaspoons vanilla extract (essence)

1¼ cups (3¾ oz/110 g) flaked coconut, toasted

TOPPING

1 cup (8 fl oz/240 ml) heavy (double) cream

2 tablespoons confectioners' (icing) sugar

½ teaspoon vanilla extract (essence)

Prepare and bake the pastry as directed and allow to cool.

For the filling, in a heavy non-aluminum saucepan, combine the granulated sugar, cornstarch and salt and whisk to mix well. In a bowl, whisk the egg yolks until blended, then gradually whisk in the milk. Gradually

whisk the egg mixture into the sugar mixture, whisking well to dissolve the cornstarch.

Place the saucepan over medium heat and cook for 4–5 minutes, stirring occasionally. Switch to a whisk occasionally to prevent lumps from forming. Continue to cook, stirring constantly and whisking occasionally, until the mixture thickens and reaches a boil, 7–9 minutes longer. Boil for 1 minute, stirring constantly, then immediately remove from heat. Stir in the butter, vanilla and 1 cup (3 oz/90 g) of the toasted coconut. Immediately pour the filling into a bowl,

press a piece of waxed (grease-proof) paper directly onto the surface and cool for 15 minutes.

For the topping, in a large bowl, whisk the cream until semisoft peaks form. Add confectioners' sugar and vanilla and whisk until soft peaks form. Cover and chill until ready to use.

Pour the filling into the cooled crust and jiggle the dish until the filling is level. Cover and chill until ready to serve. To serve, mound the topping on the pie and sprinkle with the remaining ¼ cup (¾ oz/20 g) toasted coconut. Serve immediately.

Serves 6 to 8

Macadamia Nut Cakes

4 eggs

¾ cup (6 oz/180 g) sugar

1 cup (5 oz/150 g) all-purpose (plain) flour

4 tablespoons coarsely chopped macadamia nuts

¼ cup (2 oz/60 g) unsalted butter, melted and cooled

¾ cup (6 oz/180 ml) heavy (double) cream, whipped

½ teaspoon vanilla extract (essence)

½ cup (2 oz/60 g) shredded (desiccated) coconut, lightly toasted

Preheat an oven to 350°F (180°C/Gas Mark 4). Butter and line an 8-inch (20-cm) square cake pan.

Combine the eggs and sugar in a bowl and beat until the sugar dissolves and the mixture is thick and creamy, 5–7 minutes. Sift half the flour into the egg mixture and gently fold in. Repeat with the remaining flour and 2 tablespoons of the macadamia nuts. Carefully and quickly fold in the butter.

Pour the mixture into the pan. Bake for 20 minutes, until the cake feels springy to the touch.

Invert the cake onto a wire rack to cool completely. When cool, cut into 4 squares. Cut each square horizontally in half.

In a bowl, combine the whipped cream, vanilla and the remaining 2 tablespoons of the macadamia nuts. Spread the bottom half of each square with a little of the cream mixture. Place the other half on top and spread the remaining cream over the top and edges. Sprinkle all over with the toasted shredded coconut and serve immediately.

Serves 4

Nut and Caramel
Self-saucing Pudding

¾ cup (3 oz/90 g) self-rising flour

¼ cup (1 oz/30 g) ground hazelnuts

1⅔ cups (13 fl oz/390 ml) condensed milk

1 tablespoon butter

1 teaspoon vanilla extract (essence)

½ cup (4 fl oz/120 ml) milk

1 cup (6 oz/180 g) firmly packed brown sugar

1¾ cups (14 fl oz/420 ml) boiling water

Preheat an oven to 350°F (180°C/Gas Mark 4). Butter an 8-cup (2-qt/1.9-l) capacity baking dish.

Sift the flour into a small bowl and stir in the ground hazelnuts.

Place the condensed milk in a saucepan and stir over medium heat for 10 minutes, or until thickened and slightly golden brown. Stir in the butter, vanilla and milk and continue to stir until the butter is melted. Let the milk mixture cool slightly.

Pour the milk mixture into the flour and mix well. Pour batter into the prepared dish and sift the brown sugar over the top of the pudding mixture. Carefully pour the boiling water evenly over the top of the pudding.

Bake the pudding in the oven for about 35 minutes or until firm. Allow to stand for at least 5 minutes before serving.

Serves 6

Filo Nut Pastries

1 cup (4 oz/120 g) mixed hazelnuts, pecans and walnuts

2 tablespoons honey

1 tablespoon unsalted butter

1 teaspoon ground allspice

3 sheets filo pastry

2 tablespoons unsalted butter, melted

Confectioners' (icing) sugar, for dusting

Cream or ice cream (optional), to serve

Preheat an oven to 350°F (180°C/Gas Mark 4). Butter and line a baking sheet with parchment (baking) or waxed (greaseproof) paper.

Place the mixed nuts in a food processor and process to a very coarse meal.

Combine the honey and butter in a small saucepan and stir over low heat until combined. Add to the processor, with the allspice, and process to combine.

Brush each sheet of filo with melted butter, layering one on top of the other. Cut the layered sheet lengthwise into 4 strips.

Place 2 teaspoons of the nut mixture on one corner of each strip and fold diagonally across. Continue to fold backwards and forwards diagonally across the entire pastry strip. (You should end up with a triangular packet.)

Brush each packet with a little more melted butter and place on the baking sheet. Bake for 15–20 minutes, or until the packets are puffed and golden. Sprinkle with confectioners' sugar and serve with cream or ice cream, if desired.

Makes 4

Individual Almond Tarts

PASTRY

2 cups (10 oz/300 g) all-purpose (plain) flour

2 teaspoons sugar

⅔ cup (5 oz/150 g) cold unsalted butter

I egg yolk

1–2 tablespoons ice water

I egg white, beaten

FILLING

¼ cup (2 oz/60 g) unsalted butter

⅓ cup (3 oz/90 g) sugar

I egg

I cup (4 oz/120 g) ground almonds

I teaspoon almond extract (essence)

2 tablespoons berry jam

For the pastry, combine the flour, the 2 teaspoons sugar and the butter in a food processor. Process to a coarse meal. Pulse the machine and add the egg yolk and enough of the ice water to form a cohesive mass. Remove the dough, wrap in plastic wrap and refrigerate for 30 minutes.

Preheat an oven to 300°F (150°C/Gas Mark 2).

Roll out the pastry to ⅓ inch (8 mm) thick. Cut into six 3-inch (7.5-cm) circles. Line a 6-hole cupcake pan with the pastry circles and brush each with a little beaten egg white. Refrigerate for 30 minutes.

Line each pastry circle with a round of parchment (baking) or waxed (greaseproof) paper and place baking weights (dried beans or rice) in the center of each. Bake for 10 minutes. Remove from the oven and

remove the weights and paper.
Allow to cool.

For the filling, cream the butter
and ⅓ cup (3 oz/90 g) sugar
until fluffy. Add the egg and
beat well. Fold in the ground
almonds and almond extract.
Spread each pastry shell with
about ½ teaspoon of jam and
top with the almond filling.

Bake for 10–15 minutes, until
the filling is puffed and golden.
Cool for 10 minutes in the pan,
then unmold and allow to cool
on a rack. Serve the tarts at
room temperature.

Makes 6

Glossary

The following glossary provides advice on selecting, storing, and preparing some of the ingredients used in this book.

ALCOHOLIC BEVERAGES

Amaretto is an almond-based liqueur. Armagnac is French brandy, second only to cognac, and differing rather in taste than in quality. It is aged for up to 40 years in oak barrels. Calvados is a fruit brandy made from distilled fermented apple juice. Whisky is the best substitute, but will not provide the same flavor. Cointreau is an orange-flavored liqueur from France. If Grand Marnier, another orange-flavored liqueur, is used instead you would need to cut the sugar in the recipe slightly as it is sweeter. Cream sherry is a sweetened and blended sherry and is a product of Cadiz in southern Spain. It is a type of fortified sweet wine and, in spite of a high alcohol content, deteriorates quite rapidly after opening. Frangelico is a creamy, hazelnut liqueur. Ricard liqueur is a French liqueur created from anise and has an aniseed flavor.

almonds

ALMONDS

The type of almond generally used in cooking is the sweet almond. Sweet almonds have a delicate flavor and there are many varieties. Ground almonds are commonly called for in dessert recipes. Check the label to see they have not been adulterated with another product. Blanched almonds have had their skins removed after immersion in boiling water. Almond paste is made by pounding blanched almonds into a paste and can be bought in cans or tubes from supermarkets. With the addition of sugar, and sometimes egg whites, almond paste becomes marzipan but the two cannot be interchanged in recipes. Nuts have a high fat content and will become rancid in time, particularly in a hot climate. Store shelled nuts in a cool place in an airtight container for up to 4 months, unshelled nuts for 2 months.

CANDIED (GLACÉED) FRUITS

Fruits can be crystallized by cooking them slowly in sugar syrup. The sugar acts as a preservative and the natural juices of the fruit are retained, unlike dried fruit.

CHEESES

Cottage cheese, cream cheese, farmer cheese, mascarpone, mizithra and ricotta are all types of fresh cheeses. As fresh cheeses do not have the mature flavor of ripened cheeses they are ideal for desserts. Made from a mixture of cow's cream and milk, cream cheese is appreciated

candied (glacéed) figs

for its smooth, spreadable consistency and mild, slightly tangy flavor. Mascarpone is an Italian cheese made from cream. Cottage cheese is characterized by large or small curds mixed with some milk or cream. Farmer cheese is very similar in flavor to cottage cheese, but has no curds and is usually pressed into a block form. Soft goat cheese is also a fresh cheese made from goat's milk. Ricotta is originally an Italian cheese created by heating the whey left over from making other cheeses and is usually made from sheep's milk. Mizithra is a Greek cheese very similar to the Italian ricotta. Fresh cheeses must be refrigerated and will keep for just a few days in a refrigerator once removed from their packaging.

CHOCOLATE

The following chocolate types are commonly used in baking. Unsweetened (bitter) chocolate is pure chocolate liquor with no sugar or flavoring. Unsweetened cocoa powder is pulverized pure chocolate with very little cocoa butter. With the addition of an increasing amount of sugar, the chocolate becomes bittersweet, semisweet and sweet chocolate, which are all types of plain or dark chocolate. Semisweet chocolate is the best product to use if the recipe does not call for a specific type. Milk chocolate is created by adding milk solids to chocolate liquor. White chocolate does not contain pure chocolate, so cannot be considered a true chocolate product, although it does contain cocoa butter. Store plain chocolate well wrapped in a cool, dry place for up to 12 months; milk and white chocolates will keep for up to 8 months.

COCONUT

Coconut is a favorite flavor for desserts. Processed dried coconut, shredded or flaked, normally comes in bags and can be purchased in supermarkets. Processed coconut has usually been sweetened. It will keep for several months when stored in an airtight container in a cool, dry place.

coffee beans

COFFEE

Instant coffee granules are preferred for baking because of their intense flavor and because they blend easily into batters and doughs. They will keep indefinitely if stored in an airtight container. Coffee extract (essence) is a liquid produced by freeze-drying coffee beans and is used as a flavoring. Strong fresh-brewed coffee is also used in recipes for flavoring.

COOKING FATS

Butter, margarine and solid vegetable shortening tenderize the crumb of cakes and pies. Butter and margarine are interchangeable in many recipes. However, margarine made from 100 percent vegetable oil will make a very soft dough that may require a longer chilling time to prevent the dough from spreading too much during baking. Use only regular margarine, not diet, whipped or liquid forms. Shortening is a vegetable oil-based fat manufactured to stay solid at room temperature. Butter will keep for 1 month, well wrapped in the refrigerator, or up to 6 months in the freezer. Once opened, store shortening in the refrigerator for up to a year.

cream

CREAM

Cream is classified according to the amount of milk fat it contains (from about 40 percent to about 10 percent): heavy (double) cream, light whipping cream, light (single) cream and half and half (light) cream (a mixture of milk and cream). For whipping, buy heavy cream or light whipping cream as anything lighter will not whip. Crème fraîche and sour cream are very similar products: both have been deliberately soured with the addition of a culture to convert the lactose to lactic acid. When used in baking, the lactic acid tenderizes the crumb. Keep cream in the refrigerator for as long as the label states.

DATES

Dates are fresh fruits of the date palm that are classified as soft, semi-dry or dry. Soft dates must be refrigerated and will keep for up to 3 weeks. Medjool dates are a common variety of fresh date and may have a dusting of natural sugar on their surface.

FIGS

fresh black figs

The many varieties of figs range in skin color from white to deep purple. The Black Mission fig is a small and particularly sweet variety. Fresh figs bruise easily and should be used soon after purchase.

FLOUR

All-purpose (plain) flour has a medium protein content that makes it suitable for most baking uses. Wholewheat (wholemeal) flour is coarsely milled from the entire wheat kernel; it contains more oil than other flours and will go rancid more quickly as a result. Cake (soft-wheat) flour contains cornstarch (cornflour) and is low in protein. It has been bleached, which enables it to hold more water and sugar, so a batter made with cake flour is less likely to collapse. Store white flour in an airtight container for 10–15 months; store wholemeal for up to 5 months. Refrigerate or freeze for longer storage.

SUGARS

These sweeteners add flavor and color to desserts. Dark brown sugar is a mixture of granulated sugar and molasses that adds rich, deep flavor. Light brown sugar has a less pronounced molasses flavor than dark brown sugar. Confectioners' (icing) sugar is ground and mixed with a small amount of cornstarch (cornflour) to prevent caking. Typically it is used for frostings and coatings. Granulated sugar is available in fine white crystals (most common) and superfine or caster (for frostings and meringues). Store sugars indefinitely in airtight containers in a cool, dry place.

Index

Entries in *italics* indicate illustrations and photos.